A CHILDREN'S ILLUSTRATED HISTORY

OF PRESIDENTIAL ASSASSINATION

Written by Bryan Young

A Children's Illustrated History of Presidential Assassination

Published by Silence in the Library Publishing
www.silenceinthelibrarypublishing.com

© 2014 by Bryan Young and Erin Kubinek
Written by Bryan Young
Illustrated by Erin Kubinek (and Scout Young)
Foreword by Paul S. Kemp
Cover design and interior layout by Heather Ackley
www.heatherackleyart.com
Edited by Patricia Bailey

Printed in the United States of America
First Printing: March 2014
ISBN-13: 978-0615999036

Acknowledgments

I would like to thank my family for putting up with me during the process of creating this book. I would like to thank my children especially. There would be no need for this book if it weren't for them, and Scout for specifically asking for it. I would also like to thank the team at Silence in the Library Publishing, for their support of the project: Janine Spendlove, Ron Garner, and Maggie Allen. None of this would have been possible without the support and encouragement of people like Michael Stackpole and Aaron Allston. They helped set me down the path of writing and publishing, and their contributions to anything I do will not be forgotten.

More than anything, I would like to thank the illustrator, Erin, as well. If it hadn't been for her illustrations, this book would be just a regular, old, boring history tome no one would look twice at.

–B.Y.

Thank you to my family and husband for putting up with me during this project. It was the largest work load I have had since college. I was a stressed out, emotional wreck for most of it. You are an amazing, tolerant lot. I love you.

Thank you to my coworkers that covered my shifts. You thought I was sick. I wasn't, at least not always. A couple of times I was drawing. Sorry.

To all my art teachers, and all encouragers of the pursuit of art in my life, I thank.

Heart felt thanks to our backers. You are amazing. Like "blow my gosh-darn mind" amazing.

Most of all, thanks to Bryan Young and his amazing family. It is a strange thing to be believed in so sincerely by others when you doubt yourself so ardently. But believe in me they have, and thusly this book is.

–E.K.

I want to thank Patty, Dad, and my Mom. My Dad for writing it, Patty for helping me, my Mom for kind of helping me. And Anakin, for nothing.

–S.Y.

Foreword
By Paul S. Kemp

Write the foreword to a book about politics and presidential assassinations?

Yes, count me in!

Wait, it's a children's book about politics and presidential assassinations?

Uh, you know what the word 'assassination' means, right?

You do. Okay. But it's a serious children's book about politics and presidential assassinations but interspersed with some humor?

So...children, assassinations, and humor.

Why, that hardly sounds crazy at all!

So sure, I'd love to write the foreword. After all, what could go wrong?

And by that I meant, "Wow, everything could go wrong."

And yet everything went right.

To state the obvious: I'll admit to some skepticism when Bryan first approached me about writing this foreword. The subject matter and target audience seemed a bit...well, let's call it incongruous. But then I read the book, and my skepticism vanished. It was about politics, and presidential assassinations, and history, and it was serious and sometimes funny. But most importantly (because I'm a parent of young children) it was told in a child-friendly way; not by talking down to them, but by talking up to them, and doing so in the tone that your lovable, eccentric aunt or uncle might use when spinning a bedtime yarn.

Quite a balancing act, I thought. And charmingly told.

Yet it wasn't done. Because while doing all of that it managed to be – and I'm here going to say the word a parent will love and a kid will hate -- educational.

There. I said it. The "E" word. And it's true. But the book is sneaky in its educatin' ways, because it's fun in the process. In short, it's a wonderful little book.

And boy could I have used it last year.

That's because last year my twin sons were preparing for a show-and-tell for school, and while they looked for things to talk about, they happened upon my coin collection. They eyed the Indian Head pennies with wonder. They'd only seen Lincoln pennies up to then. So they asked why Lincoln was on the penny, and I explained that he was a great president, perhaps the greatest the nation had ever seen, and that he'd been memorialized on the currency. I told them, too, that Lincoln had been assassinated. They paused, then asked, "Why?"

Why?

Think about that for a moment, and realize that the most profound question humankind has ever asked is "Why?"

Children ask it a lot.

So I tried to answer, blathering on for a while about slavery, the Civil War, secession, political disagreements generally, and a bunch of other stuff that resulted in my sons turning back to Minecraft. Oh, if I'd only had this book then. I could have turned to the Lincoln chapter, and we could have read it together. Then they'd have had a concise, engaging answer as to, "Why?"

See, "Why" is the bridge between knowledge and understanding. President Lincoln was assassinated in 1865 in Ford's Theater by John Wilkes Booth. That's knowledge. It's important. It's good to know. But knowing is not enough. Why did Booth do it? What was the historical context that gave rise to Lincoln's assassination? And how can all of that be communicated in a way a child might find engaging?

You're holding the answer in your hands right now.

One of my hobbies is reading presidential biographies. I've read quite a few. But still I learned some things reading this little book.

Quick, tell me who is George Cortelyou. Eh? Eh? Gotcha, didn't I?

Well, you'll know the answer when you read this great little book, and so will your kids. And then you and they will come away not only with many answers to the greatest question ever asked: "Why?"

Enjoy.

Paul S. Kemp is a multiple New York Times bestselling author of sword and sorcery and space opera novels, and he works very hard to make them a fun ride. He enjoys good beer, good wine, good company, and a fine scotch every now and again.

While his mind is often in the fantastical fictional worlds, his body lives in Grosse Pointe, Michigan, with his wife Jennifer, his twin sons, and his two daughters.

He is a graduate of the University of Michigan-Dearborn and the University of Michigan Law School. When he's not writing, he practices corporate law in Detroit. Yes, that does make him a tool of "the Man," for which he shall bear everlasting shame.

He hopes you enjoy his novels.

Introduction

Ever since our country established our Constitution and our representative form of government, citizens of the United States have fought and disagreed bitterly over the direction the country should take. To decide the best course of action, we hold elections and vote for those who represent our opinions best, and send them to Washington, D.C. to create and administer the laws of the land.

The single most powerful elected official in our country (and almost the entire world) is the president of the United States. The United States Government is divided into three equal branches, and the president is in charge of the Executive branch (the other two are the Judicial branch, which is the courts, and the Legislative branch, which is Congress). As the head of the Executive branch, the president is tasked with many duties. Among them, they are the Commander in Chief of the armed forces that defend our country, makes treaties with foreign nations, and appoints ambassadors, judges, and other persons in his administration to effectively run the government. The president also delivers, each year, a State of the Union address, where he or she tells Congress and the nation how things are going in the country and what he or she thinks we can do to make things better.

Through history, most presidents have won the confidence of the people of the United States in staggering majorities, meaning that most people vote for them and like the job they're doing. Sometimes though, when our country is most divided, there is a deep resentment when the person you wanted to win loses, and you become dissatisfied with the job the government is doing.

It's healthy and normal to disagree with things the president does or says, but regardless of what political party the president belongs to, the vast majority of Americans rally behind their leader and pay them the proper respect of their office.

But every so often, there are deeply disturbed individuals who don't believe in the rule of law, and they don't believe in the inherent greatness of our electoral system and wish to throw things out of balance. These people try their hardest to kill the president for a variety of reasons. In history, only four presidents have been assassinated while in office, and each time it was a national tragedy and time of great sadness.

Many other presidents have survived assassination attempts, and their stories, while no less serious, are always happier because things ended okay.

In this book, I'd love to teach you about each of the various assassination attempts made on the presidents of the United States.

My desire to do this stemmed from a trip I once took to our nation's capital, Washington, D.C., and I visited Ford's Theatre, where Abraham Lincoln was shot by an assassin. Always keenly interested in history, I was fascinated by the museum beneath the theatre that documented Lincoln's presidency and his assassination. I even took a picture of the gun used to kill him.

When I came home, I told my children about the museum and story of Lincoln's assassination, ending it with the picture of the gun.

My daughter, Scout, became obsessed. She'd heard of the assassination vaguely in school, but no one really delved deeply into the story with her. I came home from work the next day to find that she'd illustrated the entire story and tacked it on her wall; the best piece was her illustration of the small pistol that John Wilkes Booth used to perform his horrible final act.

It made me realize that kids were as interested in the darker parts of history as I was and that no one had ever given them a book about these topics in a way that made sense to them.

Until now.

I hope you enjoy this book, *A Children's Illustrated History of Presidential Assassination*.

Chapter 1

Andrew Jackson (1767-1845)

7th President of the United States

Our 7th president, Andrew Jackson, is one of the most memorable presidents from our founding era, owing to the fact that his face is on the $20 bill. Nicknamed "Old Hickory" because of his tough attitude and forceful personality, Jackson was a figure that divided the country over a variety of issues. An assassin tried to kill him on January 30, 1835. He was the first president to be threatened with assassination.

ANDREW JACKSON

Old Hickory

He was a rich owner of slaves from Tennessee, and fought in many duels, even killing some of his opponents.

His father died before his birth and his mother raised him and his two brothers with the help of relatives. His oldest brother, Hugh, enlisted in a regiment during the American War for Independence and died of heat stroke at the Battle of Stono Ferry. At 13 years old, Andrew Jackson volunteered with a local militia to fight against the British in the Revolutionary War with his older brother, Robert. Because of their young age, they were made couriers, but they were quickly captured by enemy soldiers and almost starved to death in their captivity. At one time, a British officer tried forcing Jackson to polish his boots. The young boy willfully refused and the soldier slashed at the boy with his sword, scarring his hand and his head for the rest of his life.

Before they were freed from the British prison, both Jackson boys got sick with small pox. Andrew's brother, Robert, died of the disease shortly after their release.

After securing the release of her children, Jackson's mother went to work trying to do the same for her nephews when she contracted cholera and also died.

At the age of 14, Andrew Jackson, already a hardened veteran of the Revolutionary War, became an orphan. He forever blamed the British for the death of his family and maintained a fierce hatred of them.

Relying on his intelligence, Jackson became a frontier lawyer with little education. He was so smart and popular in the state of Tennessee he was a delegate for the state's constitutional convention in 1795, the first congressman from Tennessee, and after that a senator. After just one year as senator, Jackson resigned to work closer to home, taking a judgeship, then got elected as the major general in command of the state militia. The man he beat, a career general and twenty years his senior, was furious at his loss, leading the two men to fight in a duel in the streets of Knoxville.

One famous duel Jackson fought was in 1806 over a misunderstanding involving a horse race. He dueled by pistol with a man named Charles Dickinson. Dickinson fired first and scored a hit in Jackson's chest, but Jackson refused to let that matter. He aimed slowly and carefully, pulled the trigger of the pistol, and killed his opponent. He spent the rest of his life with Dickinson's bullet lodged in his middle.

Jackson distinguished himself as a military leader during the War of 1812, fighting the British, the Spanish and the Native Americans (then called "Indians").

After winning Florida for the United States and being elected its first governor, he resigned and moved back to Tennessee, where his friends were plotting to promote him for the presidency.

When he was elected president in 1829, he was known for many divisive things. One was getting rid of the National Bank, feeling that it concentrated the power of money and government into the hands of the elite rich. He also called repeatedly for the abolishment of the Electoral College, wanting to put the power of presidential election directly in the hands of the people. He was also the only president to completely pay off the national debt. The most divisive policy of President Jackson, though, was his idea of "Indian Removal." It was his policy that Native Americans should be removed completely from areas the United States wanted to settle, and he was responsible for starting "The Trail of Tears."

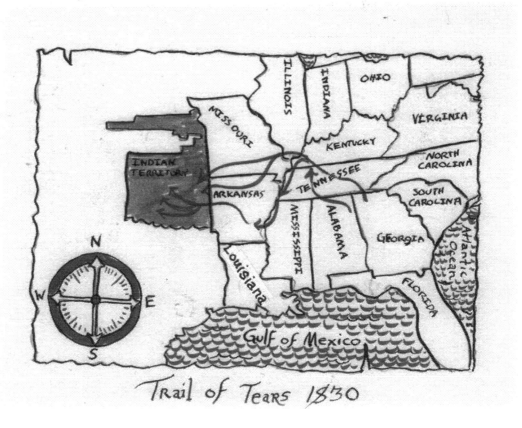

Trail of Tears 1830

The Trail of Tears was the name given to the forced relocation of Native Americans after the passage of the Indian Removal Act of 1830. It forced Native American tribes to walk to their new homeland in "Indian Territory" which includes most of present day Oklahoma. Andrew Jackson saw to it that the military forced each of the Native American tribes from their homes so white settlers could cultivate the land.

Even though he presided over many policies that had vigorous opponents, none of these were the reason Richard Lawrence tried to kill the president. Lawrence was a simple house painter who became mentally ill from exposure to chemicals in the paint he used.

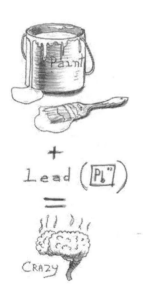

He began to have delusions, thinking things that simply weren't true. He began to dress in bright colorful clothes, grew a mustache, and quit his job, telling those around him that he had no need for money since the American government owed him money, and they would pay him shortly.

In his delirium, he became convinced that President Jackson was the final barrier standing in the way of taking his rightful place as Richard III. Once Jackson was dead, he could receive the money the government owed him, and he would be the King of England once more.

RICHARD LAWRENCE

He bought two small Deringer pistols, and began to stalk the president, following his every move.

On the morning of January 30, 1835, the president was attending the funeral of South Carolina Representative Warren R. Davis at the United States Capitol. Lawrence tried to get close enough to shoot the president on his way into the funeral, but was unable to do so. Instead, he waited until Jackson was leaving and made his move.

Jackson was leaving the Capitol through the East Portico when Lawrence struck, firing his first pistol...

...but it misfired!

Pulling his second pistol, he fired again...

...but it misfired, too!

Not one to take such actions lightly, Jackson hit Lawrence with his cane, chasing him around and hitting him until the onlookers could restrain the would-be assassin. Fortunately for everyone, Congressman Davy Crockett, hero of the frontier, was there and was able to subdue Lawrence with the other onlookers.

Even though Davy Crockett disagreed strongly with President Jackson's policies, he still did his part to ensure no harm befell the president.

Richard Lawrence was brought to court and deemed not guilty for reasons of insanity and spent the rest of his natural life in mental institutions.

The Smithsonian Institute still has the guns that Lawrence used in the first attempt on a president's life. In the 1930s, they test-fired the guns to see if they worked. They both shot perfectly on the first try. Historians believe the guns misfired initially because of the moisture in the air on the day of the funeral. Mathematicians have since determined that the odds of both guns not going off on the day of the attempt were 1 in 125,000.

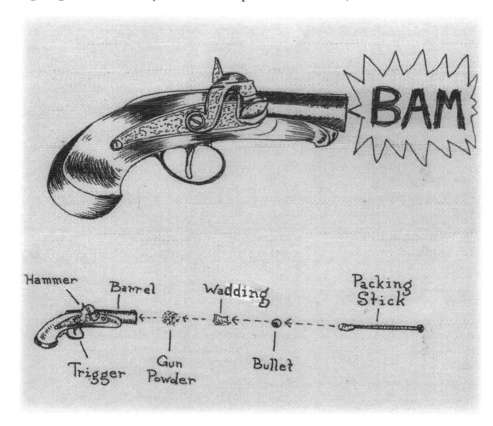

Though there was no reason or evidence to suspect that Jackson's political rivals were behind the assassination attempt, Jackson himself was convinced that Lawrence was hired by his opponents to kill him. Jackson's vice president (and future president), Martin Van Buren, believed the suspicions and, from that point forward, carried loaded pistols with him whenever he visited the Senate.

Scout's Presidential Portrait

Chapter 2

Abraham Lincoln (1809-1865)

16th President of the United States

Believed by many to have been the greatest president the United States has ever had, Abraham Lincoln started from very humble beginnings as a laborer on the frontier. As a boy, he worked his family's land, became an axeman, splitting rails for fences, and was renowned for his strength and wrestling abilities.

ABRAHAM LINCOLN

Because of his reputation, he was even challenged to a wrestling match by the leader of the Clary's Grove Boys, a notorious band of ruffians.

Reading with every spare moment, he taught himself the skills necessary to become a lawyer and legislator.

Lincoln entered politics as a Whig (an early political party), and in 1846 he was elected to the U.S. House of Representatives where he served a single two-year term. He campaigned on a desire to prevent the spread of legalized slavery in new territories. He was deeply against slavery, but didn't feel the government had the right to take away the rights of southern states where the practice was already well-established.

Lincoln promised to serve only one term as congressman, and dedicated his political efforts to ensuring the election of fellow Whig Zachary Taylor to the presidency before returning to his private legal practice.

He came back to the political scene in the 1850s, outraged by legislation called the Kansas-Nebraska Act that would open the door to allowing slavery in new states in the West.

By 1858, Lincoln was in the running to represent Illinois in the United States Senate. Back in the those days, people didn't directly elect senators, they were chosen by the state legislatures. Lincoln spent that year campaigning against a gentleman named Stephen Douglas. They held seven debates that have been called the most famous debates in American political history. The main topic of their debates was slavery, and each of the candidates were on different sides of the issue. Lincoln claimed Douglas was part of a national conspiracy to nationalize slavery. Douglas made the claim that Lincoln was too radical for believing that the Declaration of Independence, stating that all men were created equal, applied to slaves as well as whites.

Lincoln ended up losing the election, but took transcripts from his debates with Senator Douglas and published them in a book. The popularity of the book is one of the major factors that led to his nomination for the presidency two years later in 1860.

After winning the Republican Party nomination in their first convention ever, Abraham Lincoln went on to win the election by a narrow margin. Southern states were convinced that President-elect Lincoln would be intent on taking their slaves, so they made clear their intentions to secede (break apart) from the Union by the time of Lincoln's inauguration in March of 1861, even going so far as to elect their own president, Jefferson Davis, in the middle of February.

The sitting president at that time, James Buchanan, and the upcoming president, both believed secession was illegal, and that the United States must be kept whole. This attitude didn't make the southern states happy.

On February 11, 1861, Abraham Lincoln got on a train in Illinois, planning a railroad tour of seventy towns and cities along the rail route to Washington, D.C., ending with his first inauguration.

Due to the potential for violence against the president-elect, the railroad company hired Allan Pinkerton (of the world famous Pinkerton Detective Agency) to protect Honest Abe on his momentous journey.

Pinkerton was convinced of a "Baltimore Plot" of angry Americans who wanted to kill the incoming president on his way through Maryland's capital city. In Baltimore, Lincoln and his entourage would have to switch train lines for the rest of the journey to Washington. It was expected that a crowd would be assembled and rumors spoke of a group of would-be assassins, each armed with easily concealed knives. Since they would be dressed just like everyone else, the threat could come from anywhere.

Pinkerton took no chances.

They planned their trip through Baltimore and into Washington so that they would arrive in the middle of the night. Pinkerton ordered telegraph lines into and out of the city cut. Lincoln's train moved in secret, silently running the rails led by mules instead of a steam engine. Disguised in a scotch-cap and long cloak, Lincoln switched trains and made it to Washington under the cover of darkness.

As soon as the president-elect made it safely through Baltimore, Pinkerton sent a one line telegram to the president of the railroad that read, "Plums delivered nuts safely."

The next day, the crowd in Baltimore, full of alleged assassins, arrived to greet the next president of the United States, including Lincoln's wife and children, only to find that he'd already passed through the night previous.

Lincoln's opponents tried using this against him, saying that he was an usurper to the post of president, and a coward for stealing into our nation's capital in the middle of the night like a thief.

After being sworn into office, President Lincoln directed much of his address to the fact that he wanted to see the nation remain in one piece, and that he wasn't trying to steal anyone's property. "We are not enemies, but friends. We must not be enemies."

Through peace talks and negotiation, it was clear that the leaders of the South had no intention of remaining members of the Union, but to President Lincoln, this idea was intolerable.

The American Civil War began on April 12, 1861, the month after Abraham Lincoln became the president of the United States. The Confederacy attacked Fort Sumter in South Carolina, which was a Union military installation. The Confederacy called for the abandonment of the fort, instead President Lincoln sent the fort new supplies, telling the South quite clearly that the North was ready to fight.

The North and South fought each other bitterly, each side working hard to take the other's capital city. Families were divided, brothers were killing brothers, and it was the darkest time in American history.

On January 1, 1863, Abraham Lincoln issued an executive order known as the Emancipation Proclamation. The proclamation said that slaves in the rebelling states of the Confederacy would be freed by the advancing Union Army. This further enraged the South, reignited anti-slavery sentiment, and granted freedom to millions of slaves.

To ensure that slavery would be abolished in every state, not just those states that rebelled, President Lincoln pushed for the Thirteenth Amendment to the Constitution. This would abolish slavery everywhere in the United States in a way that couldn't be challenged in court or overturned.

In 1864, the president won a narrow reelection against General George McLellan, his former top general during the war. Though he won by more than half a million votes, Abraham Lincoln was convinced he'd lose the election. He was sworn into office once more on March 4, 1865. He concluded his second inaugural address with the following statement, wishing a speedy end to the war and a healing of the wounds that tore America apart, "With malice toward none, with charity for all, with firmness in the right as God gives us to see the right, let us strive on to finish the work we are in, to bind up the nation's wounds, to care for him who shall have borne the battle and for his widow and his orphan, to do all which may achieve and cherish a just and lasting peace among ourselves and with all nations."

On April 1, 1865, less than a month after Abraham Lincoln began his second term as president, General Ulysses S. Grant (who would become the 18th president of the United States) outflanked the Confederacy's major remaining forces (led by General Robert E. Lee) in the Battle of Five Forks. This forced Lee into a retreat that ended with his surrender of the Confederacy in the village Appomattox Court House, Virginia on April 9, 1865.

Less than a month after his second inaugural address, the speedy end to the war that Lincoln hoped for came.

The tale of President Lincoln's assassination begins just before the end of the war. In March of 1865, a 25 year old stage actor named John Wilkes Booth decided he would kidnap the president and ransom him for the release of Confederate soldiers held prisoner in the North.

Booth was deeply unhappy with the North's policies on slavery, hated Lincoln with a fiery passion, and acted as a Confederate spy in Maryland. His own family was as deeply divided as the country; his older brother even banished him from his home because of his hatred of Lincoln and the North.

Further isolated, he assembled a team of people sympathetic to his views and spent much time and money plotting the kidnapping. With his team in place, Booth was ready to carry out his plot on March 17, 1865. The president would be attending a play familiar to the conspirators. They hid out on the road, laying in wait for the president, so they could overpower him and whisk him across the border and deliver him to the Confederacy...

...but the president never came.

His plans changed at the last moment and he actually attended a reception at the National Hotel where Booth himself was staying.

Soon enough, the war ended, but Booth was still completely invested in his cause. He wanted to reignite the fires of the South and burn the whole of the North to the ground. His plan shifted from kidnapping to assassination.

On April 11, 1865, just two days after the South surrendered, John Wilkes Booth attended a speech given by President Lincoln at the White House. The president was encouraging the enfranchisement of freed slaves. That meant freed slaves would be able to vote in elections and become true and proper citizens of the United States.

For someone as racist and angry as John Wilkes Booth, this was not welcome news. A few days later, he wrote in a letter to his mother that he had to do something decisive and great, otherwise his dream of a once more rising South would be lost forever.

On the morning of April 14, 1865, John Wilkes Booth went to Ford's Theatre in Washington, D.C. to check his mail. Since he was friendly with the owners, he learned that the president would that night be attending the play Our American Cousin.

Booth left and went immediately to work on his plan.

He called his original kidnapping team back to action. His bold and decisive move called not for one killing, but four. The plan always called for Booth to shoot Lincoln, but he intended to knife General Grant, who was supposed to be seeing the play with the president, as well.

He assigned a man named George Atzerodt to kill Vice President Andrew Johnson and a man named Lewis Powell to kill Secretary of State William Seward. Their plan was to destroy the leadership of the Union in one night, plunging the country into chaos, and allowing the South to take the country back once and for all.

GEORGE ATZERODT

LEWIS POWELL

Fortunately for General Grant, he declined the invitation to watch the play with President Lincoln at the insistence of his wife, who didn't get along with the first lady, Mary Todd Lincoln.

The others targeted for assassination that night were also spared their lives. Lewis Powell managed to stab Seward, who was bedridden, recovering from a broken jaw and arm. Explaining to the Seward's butler that he was a doctor bringing medicine to the ailing secretary of state, Powell forced his way into the house, knocked out Seward's son, shoved his daughter aside, and began stabbing at his target.

The splint the doctors had fashioned to heal Seward's jaw may have been the only thing that saved him. He suffered only a slashed cheek and no mortal wounds. Others came to the secretary's aid, fighting with Powell and chasing him away. He stabbed one young man on his way out, paralyzing him for life.

ANDREW JOHNSON

For his part, George Atzerodt was to shoot the vice president at his hotel. Atzerodt had checked out the room directly above Vice President Johnson, then had gone to the bar to wait for his target. Instead of performing his assigned task, he got drunk at the bar and wandered into the night, roaming the streets of Washington before throwing his knife away and checking into another hotel, where he then passed out, drunk.

The president and Mrs. Lincoln, accompanied by Major Henry Rathbone and his fiancee, Clara Harris, arrived at Ford's Theatre late. The four of them went up to the presidential box to watch the play. It was said that Abraham Lincoln spoke his last words to his wife in response to a question she asked.

"What will Miss Harris think of me hanging on you so?" she asked him.

"She won't think anything about it."

He spent the rest of his life silently enjoying the play.

Outside his box was a policeman named John Frederick Parker. Parker was a known drunk and had been previously charged with dereliction of duty, so it came as no surprise to find that during the intermission, he had left his post. He went to a nearby tavern to have a drink with the president's footman and coachman.

Since Booth was a famous actor and regular at Ford's Theatre, his arrival at the theatre aroused no suspicion.

He snuck up the stairs to the presidential box and waited outside the door Parker should have been guarding.

FORD'S THEATER

Clutching his Deringer, he stepped into the room just outside the box, waiting for the funniest line in the play to be spoken, hoping the laughter would mask the sound of his gunshot and aid in his escape.

The line was spoken, Booth stepped into the presidential box and then shot President Lincoln in the back of the head behind his left ear. Slumping forward in his chair, a mortally wounded Lincoln was caught by his wife, who then screamed.

As soon as he heard the gunshot, Major Rathbone sprung into action, trying to apprehend Booth. Ready with a knife, the assassin stabbed the major in the arm and slashed at his head, allowing him just enough time to leap from the box to the stage from which he yelled, "Sic semper tyranis!"

Sic semper tyranis, is latin for "thus always to tyrants."

As he fled the stage, Mrs. Lincoln continued screaming and Major Rathbone shouted, "Stop that man!"

Suddenly, everyone knew what was happening, and chaos ensued.

A few men tried chasing Booth across the stage, but he reached his horse behind the theatre, smashed the man holding it for him with the handle of his knife, kicked another man and was on his way, disappearing into the night.

A young army surgeon named Charles Leale was attending the play that night and made his way up to the presidential box, hoping he could help save the president's life. Two more doctors from the audience, Charles Taft and Albert King, arrived on the scene and were able to keep the president breathing. They decided to move him across the street to the boarding house owned by William Peterson.

The surgeon general of the United States arrived, as well as other doctors. They were able to keep President Lincoln alive through most of the night, but there was nothing more they could do. At 7:22 a.m. on April 15, 1865, President Lincoln passed away.

"Now he belongs to the ages," said Edwin Stanton, the secretary of war, when the president died.

Major Rathbone's injuries suffered in trying to stop Booth weren't life threatening, but he did have his own problems stemming from the assassination just a few years later. While living in Germany as the consul of Hanover, his mental state declined rapidly. So consumed with guilt and grief over his inability to save President Lincoln, he went crazy, killing his wife Clara on July 11, 1867. He tried to kill their children, then tried to stab himself to death. He lived until 1911 in a German asylum for the criminally insane.

John Wilkes Booth was a fugitive on the run from the law for the next 12 days.

At some point during his initial escape, Booth broke his leg and needed to be put in a splint and on crutches. Many people say he broke his leg when he leapt from the stage, but some historians think that was simply Booth exaggerating the tale of his flight. Some think he most likely broke it during his ride out of town after his horse threw him.

After spending a day at the home of Doctor Samuel Mudd, he hired a guide to help him cross the Potomac River. On April 24th, he found himself at the tobacco farm owned by a Confederate sympathizer named Richard Garrett.

There Booth remained with an accomplice until April 26th, 1865 when Union soldiers arrived on the scene and surrounded the barn where the president's assassin was hiding.

The soldiers called for Booth to surrender, but he shouted back at them, "I will not be taken alive!"

When they heard this, the soldiers simply set fire to the barn.

Booth headed for the back door, a gun in each hand, but he never had a chance to fire either one. A soldier named Boston Corbett had snuck behind the barn and shot Booth in the neck. The soldiers carried Booth to the steps of the barn where he told them, "Tell my mother I die for my country."

Then, unable to move, he gazed at the soldiers and uttered his final words. "Useless... Useless..."

The rest of Booth's gang were caught by the end of the month. Most were sentenced to death by hanging and were executed on July 7, 1865.

Abraham Lincoln was mourned throughout the country, North and South. He had kept the Union together and worked hard to ensure a fair and gentle reconstruction of the tattered South as far as his short time allowed.

Andrew Johnson became the 17th president of the United States on the day of Lincoln's death, the day after the assassination.

The president's body was brought to the White House and held in state in the East Room and then in the Capitol Rotunda from April 19th to April 21st. Then, his body was put on a train that travelled from across the country. For the next three weeks, his funeral train brought his body to major cities throughout the North where huge memorials were held, attended by hundreds of thousands of Americans, mourning the loss of their president.

Over the years, Abraham Lincoln has been remembered as one of the greatest presidents the United States has ever had. He kept our country together when it was in danger of being torn in half, and ended the enslavement of millions of Americans. We can only guess how much better our world would be today if John Wilkes Booth hadn't cut Lincoln's life so tragically short that dark April evening in 1865, just over a month into his second term.

Scout's Presidential Portrait

Scout's Assassination Interpretation

Chapter 3

James A. Garfield (1831-1881)

20th President of the United States

    Like many presidents in his era, James Garfield was a military veteran of the Civil War, but he was not a professional soldier. He began his career as a teacher, instructing students in classical languages and then later as a principal. Wishing for a change of pace, he switched to being a lawyer in 1859 and was admitted by the Ohio Bar in 1860.

JAMES GARFIELD

Garfield is a remarkable man in that, except for his position in the Union Army, he never actually sought any position or an office. When he became an Ohio state senator in 1859, the party asked him to serve and elected him without any campaigning on Garfield's part.

In 1862, after distinguishing himself during the war, he was approached by friends to run for the U.S. Congress in Ohio's 19th district. He didn't feel it was appropriate to use his military position to advance his political career, so he told his friends that he'd be happy to serve if he was elected, but he would not seek the post out on his own.

He beat his opponent handily and began his first of ten terms in that post.

In 1879, the Ohio Legislature chose Garfield to represent them in the Senate, but things were going to change for him drastically at the Republican Convention in 1880. Former President Grant was hoping to win the party nomination for an unprecedented third term in the presidency, but many in the party were uncomfortable with that idea. Other candidates appeared, all wanting to unseat then-President Rutherford B. Hayes. Garfield spoke eloquently as a voice of reason through the process, watching each vote come back in a deadlock. Suddenly, even though he wasn't even in the running, his name was suggested as a compromise candidate and he won the party nomination and later the presidency.

Back in those days, every person with a position in the federal government (about 100,000 at that time) expected to lose their job, and every time a new president entered the White House, Washington was besieged with people looking for jobs. After his election, Garfield was drowning in office-seekers, and he set out to make civil service reform one of the keystones of his legacy. His inaugural address promised to work hard to ensure that African Americans were given all the rights due to them as American citizens.

Though the president didn't know it at the time, at some point in June of 1881, a man named Charles Guiteau, a lawyer and ardent Republican supporter, was stalking him with a .44 revolver through Lafayette Square and other areas around Washington and the White House.

Guiteau had come to Washington seeking a job, along with thousands of others. He came back to the White House day after day, demanding a job or post in the cabinet, feeling he was owed for something. He insisted that a speech he wrote (titled Grant vs. Hancock and retitled to Garfield vs. Hancock after the election) was the deciding factor in Garfield's bid for the presidency.

Finally, on May 14, 1881, after repeatedly rejecting Guiteau's absurd request to be the consul of Paris, Secretary of State James Blaine told him to leave and never come back.

Guiteau left to borrow $15 with which to purchase a gun and began his stalking.

His first opportunity to shoot President Garfield presented itself on a rail platform, where the president was seeing his sick wife off. Guiteau decided he didn't want to upset the first lady, so he opted to wait until later.

The assassin was given his next opportunity on July 2, 1881, when the president was on his way to deliver a speech. Guiteau had been waiting for him at the Baltimore and Potomac Railroad Station. Accompanied by his two sons James and Harry, Secretary of State Blaine, and Abraham Lincoln's son Robert Todd Lincoln, Garfield walked by Guiteau. Guiteau stepped behind them and fired two shots at the president.

"My God, what is this?" the president exclaimed after being shot. One bullet grazed Garfield's arm, the other entered his back.

Guiteau saved the government the sort of prolonged manhunt John Wilkes Booth had caused. He surrendered immediately, telling the officers, "I am a stalwart of the stalwarts. Arthur is president now!"

Doctors worked hard to remove the bullet from Garfield's back, which may have been the thing that actually killed him. They poked and prodded with unsterilized fingers looking for the bullet so they could remove it. Alexander Graham Bell even created a magnetic device that would hopefully locate the bullet, though the metal springs in the mattress interfered with the device.

Garfield didn't die immediately. He stayed alive, fevered and deathly ill with infection from the gunshot wounds, bedridden at the White House.

An unnamed navy engineer and a man named Simon Newcomb invented their own early air conditioner when they installed an air blower over six tons of ice to keep the ailing president cool and comfortable in the increasingly oppressive heat of Washington.

President Garfield held on as long as he could, but on September 19, 1881, more than three months after he'd been shot, he suffered a massive heart attack and passed away at the age of 49.

His final words were, "My work is done."

Doctors tried reviving him, but he was beyond hope. Modern doctors are convinced that if they had today's technology, President Garfield would have survived his assassination attempt.

Once the president finally succumbed to his wounds, the government charged the assassin with murder. Guiteau tried to plead insanity, but was found guilty and of sound mind, and he was hanged on June 30, 1882.

He literally danced his way to the gallows.

Pieces of his brain are still on display at museums in Philadelphia and Maryland.

President Garfield's body went first to our nation's capitol, then to Ohio, where it was buried and memorialized. Like President Lincoln before him, he traveled by train and memorial services were held along the way, but the largest was in Ohio where more than 150,000 came to mourn him.

But his legacy didn't die there.

Many politicians in Washington blamed the president's death on the nature of political office-seeking. It was a crazed office-seeker that shot Garfield, so something had to be done to reform the system. Senator George Pendleton from Ohio created the Pendleton Civil Service Reform Act which made it illegal to fire federal employees for political reasons. Federal employees could no longer be hired based solely on political party, each of them would have to complete an exam to prove competency in their future job.

This act was signed into law in 1883 by President Chester A. Arthur, who took over the remainder of President Garfield's term.

Scout's Presidential Portrait

Chapter 4

William McKinley (1843-1901)

25th President of the United States

As an 18 year old man, William McKinley volunteered for the Union Army as a private and fought in many battles before being promoted to brevet major when the Civil War ended. His unit disbanded, and he returned to his home in Poland, Ohio and began to study law.

WILLIAM MCKINLEY

He moved about until he opened a law practice in Canton, Ohio in 1867. McKinley entered politics quite indirectly. When his old friend and mentor from the war, Rutherford B. Hayes, was running for governor of Ohio, McKinley began making speeches around town on his behalf. Hayes was successful, and McKinley ended up edging closer and closer to politics. First, he won an election as a prosecuting attorney for Stark County, Ohio, then as a congressman in Ohio's 17th congressional district. While he campaigned for Congress in 1876, he also campaigned to get his friend, Governor Hayes, elected president. Both were successful.

McKinley served as a congressman most of the time between 1876 and 1892, fighting for protective tariffs for American industry. Tariffs are taxes paid on items being imported to or exported from the country. The Tariff Act of 1890 (referred to as the McKinley Tariff Act) was written by William McKinley, and it raised taxes on items coming into the United States. It meant that items manufactured inside of America were cheaper to produce and cheaper to buy, spurring the American economy.

At the time (and even today), tariffs were very controversial and hotly debated. Most of the McKinley Tariff Act was overturned when Democrats took over the House and Senate just four years later.

Before he even left his post as a congressman, McKinley ran for, and won, the post of governor of Ohio, which had helped his mentor Rutherford B. Hayes ascend to the presidency. Because the governor of Ohio could only suggest possible legislation and had no veto power over state lawmakers, the position wasn't one of much power. But because Ohio was a swing state (meaning it wasn't reliably Republican or Democrat) the governor held a lot of influence over the course of national politics, giving McKinley a very loud voice on a national stage.

Using this position to aid many other influential Republican lawmakers into office, this was the perfect stepping stone to launch McKinley into the presidency.

The major issue of the 1896 presidential election was the Gold Standard. The Gold Standard was a system of money that fixed the value of a dollar to a specific amount of gold. You could trade paper money for gold coins and back again at a fixed rate, and the entire system of money was based on this relationship. McKinley wanted to keep us on the Gold Standard. His opponent, William Jennings Bryan (the youngest man ever to run for president for a major party) wanted us to shift to a free silver policy. That meant they wanted to use silver as the base standard of currency, but allow it to be exchanged with gold at a 16 to 1 ratio. That meant you would be able to get 1 ounce of gold for 16 ounces of silver. Since silver was easier to attain, it would make debts easier to pay for poorer Americans.

Since this would be bad for the banks and the rich (whose loans would be repaid back at lower values), they backed McKinley and gave him all the money he needed to campaign and win the election.

One of the major issues of McKinley's first term as president was the Spanish-American War. The citizens of Cuba were fighting for their independence against Spain, much the same way America had fought for her independence against the British. The American public wanted to come to Cuba's aid, but McKinley was skeptical, offering only to send the USS Maine to the coast of Cuba, only to have it destroyed.

The American public demanded war, even though the cause of the Maine's destruction had yet to be determined. Still set against the war, McKinley deferred the decision to Congress, who declared war on Spain, whether McKinley wanted it or not.

The American Navy began engaging the Spanish, and ground troops were sent to secure Cuba and the other Spanish holdings, Puerto Rico and the Philippines. Because Spain was so far away from the United States and its outlying territories, it had a difficult time keeping up with America, who soon won the war.

President McKinley won reelection in 1900 (against William Jennings Bryan again) by an even larger margin than the 1896 election.

To some, President McKinley was a symbol of greed for the banks and industry, working to protect them and their interests above those of the workers. To others, he was a stalwart protecting the hard working Americans who had invested their money wisely. During his final tour of the country before his assassination, he was giving public speeches, advocating for "reciprocity treaties." Those were treaties with other countries that would ensure foreign markets were available for American manufacturers to sell their goods.

During his tour, McKinley would give receptions after his speeches, meeting people and shaking the hands of the public. George Cortelyou, McKinley's personal secretary and chief of staff, grew worried about news from Europe where anarchists had assassinated other world leaders. He felt McKinley could very well be in danger and shouldn't be participating in public receptions after speeches. He tried removing them from the president's schedule, but McKinley refused to allow it. Instead, Cortelyou simply arranged more security, hoping that would be enough.

LEON CZOLGOSZ

Cortelyou wasn't the only person affected by the news of the assassinations. A young American of Polish descent named Leon Czolgosz (pronounced chol-goze) learned of the assassination of King Umberto I of Italy at the hands of an anarchist and grew inspired. Czolgosz was himself an anarchist, believing that McKinley was an enemy of the people, using his power to prop up the rich and the elite on the backs of working people across the country.

King UMBERTo I

Because of this great injustice in society that Czolgosz saw, and because of the inspiration of other anarchists in the world, he felt that assassinating President McKinley would be a heroic act that would strike a blow for the oppressed masses everywhere.

Knowing that the president would be speaking at the Pan-American Exposition (a world's fair) in Buffalo, New York, Czolgosz set out for Buffalo with the intent to kill the president.

On September 5th, the armed anarchist attended a speech being given by McKinley. During the speech, Czolgosz did his best to find a moment to shoot McKinley, but from the ground below the dais and podium he couldn't be sure he'd hit his target, so he waited until the time was right.

On the next day, McKinley stood in a receiving line in the Temple of Music, shaking hands with and talking to the public. With his gun wrapped in a handkerchief, Czolgosz got into the line, ignored by security, and waited for his turn with the president. When Czolgosz got to the front of the line, McKinley extended his hand for a handshake, but his hand was slapped away. Raising the hidden gun with his other hand, Czolgosz fired two shots into the president.

The first shot was deflected by a button on the president's shirt or coat, but the second went into his stomach.

The crowd turned into a mob, grabbing Czogolsz and beating him savagely. But the wounded president saved his life, calling out, "Don't hurt him, boys!"

McKinley pleaded for them to simply capture the "poor, misguided fellow."

To many, McKinley's reaction to being shot was a direct contradiction to the image of him Czolgosz held. Here was Czolgosz, trying to kill this man as being an enemy of the people, but instead the man he shot was his only defender, concerned about his welfare.

The assassin was taken to jail and McKinley was taken (by electric ambulance!) to the hospital on the grounds of the Exposition. Unfortunately, the hospital wasn't much of a hospital and had only attended to the minor wounds of those at the fair. There were no qualified doctors, either, only nurses and interns. A message was sent to the best doctor in the city (and medical director of the Exposition), Dr. Roswell Park, who was in Niagara Falls performing surgery. In the middle of the operation, he was interrupted and told he was needed urgently in Buffalo at the Exposition. He said that he couldn't leave the surgery even if it was the president of the United States who needed him. When he learned it really was the president who needed him, he still wouldn't leave.

A number of doctors who happened to be nearby arrived to help at the Exposition hospital, including a gynecologist named Matthew Mann. Mann was chosen by Cortelyou to perform the surgery to remove the bullet and repair any damage to the president's internal organs.

While lying on the operating table, waiting to be knocked out for the surgery, McKinley said of his assassin, "He didn't know, poor fellow, what he was doing. He couldn't have known."

The surgery was difficult for many reasons. For one, the hospital didn't have the proper tools for the surgery. For two, the operating theatre wasn't wired with electric lights. The shooting happened in the late afternoon, and the sunlight was dwindling.

Mann inserted his fingers into the president's abdomen, searching for the bullet, but it seemed to have vanished. A brand new X-ray machine was on display at the fair, a new invention of Thomas Edison's, but they decided not to use it on the president for fear that there might be side-effects to using the new technology. Giving it his best guess, Mann surmised that the bullet must have lodged in the president's back muscles and proceeded to sew him back up.

The surgery was deemed a success and McKinley was brought to the Milburn House, where he was staying in Buffalo for the Exposition, to recover.

McKinley was hale and hearty and gave all appearances that he was recovering from his wounds. He met with his wife and chief of staff and was eager to hear news of how well liked his speech at the Exposition was.

Vice President Theodore Roosevelt was furious when he learned that the maximum sentence Czogolsz could receive for the attempted murder of the president was ten years in prison. Roosevelt had been called back from his vacation after the attempt and left again for the Adirondack Mountains after seeing that McKinley would recover.

McKinley grew stronger for a couple of days, after eating some broth and receiving nutritive enemas.

But, on the morning of September 13, 1901, seven days after being shot, McKinley collapsed. McKinley spent the day in bed, mostly unconscious. By evening, he said, "It is useless gentlemen. I think we ought to have a prayer."

He spent the day and night attended by friends and family. Businessman Mark Hanna, who had financed McKinley's political campaigns, tears in his eyes over his dying friend, was the one to discover that McKinley had passed away at about 2:15 a.m., on September 14th.

A park ranger had been sent earlier in the day to find Vice President Roosevelt in the mountains to inform him of the news. As soon as he heard, he raced to Buffalo, first on horseback and then by train so he could be sworn in as the 26th president of the United States.

After doctors performed an autopsy, they learned that McKinley had been killed by infection and gangrene that originated in the lining of his stomach. Gangrene is a deadly disease that happens when large amounts of body tissue dies.

Dr. Mann's treatment of the president was criticized widely as malpractice.

Since McKinley had died, Czolgosz was charged with murder. Because he was an anarchist and completely against all forms of authority, he refused to talk to his legal defense team, the judge, or anyone else in a position of authority. His trial began on September 24, 1901, with his defense lawyers claiming he was clearly insane, but since he wouldn't speak it was difficult to prove.

Czolgosz was sentenced to death, and on October 29, 1901, he was electrocuted to death. His last words regarding his crime were, "I killed the president because he was the enemy of the good people – the good working people. I am not sorry for my crime."

Then, as the guards were strapping him into the chair, he said with some difficulty, "I am only sorry I could not get to see my father."

Scout's Presidential Portrait

Scout's Assassination Interpretation

Chapter 5

Theodore Roosevelt (1858-1919)

26th President of the United States

One of the four faces carved into the stone of Mount Rushmore, Theodore Roosevelt was known as an exuberant fellow, an avid hunter and outdoorsman, and wealthy man's man.

This image of him doesn't seem to match his childhood. Born to a wealthy New York family, he was a sickly boy with asthma who was home schooled. His passion was natural history, and he spent his days studying the outdoors. As he got older, he engaged in more physical activities to make up for his lack of them in childhood. At Harvard University, where he studied biology, he was a boxer.

After graduating, he got married, wrote some history books, and was elected to the New York State Assembly.

THEODORE ROOSEVELT

On Valentine's Day of 1884, just two days after the birth of his daughter, Alice, tragedy struck the Roosevelt family. While at work in the New York Legislature, working hard to get a reform bill passed, he was summoned home. His mother had passed away, a victim of typhoid fever. Later that day, his wife, Alice Lee, died of a severe kidney illness known as Bright's disease.

The death of his wife and his mother on the same day was devastating. In a severe depression, he left his newborn daughter in the care of his sister, abandoned politics, and lit out for the Dakota territories. There, he lived as a rancher and a sheriff, spending the rest of his free time reading and writing history books.

After a blizzard in late 1885 wiped out his prized herd of cattle, Roosevelt felt it was time to come back home to New York. He re-entered life as a politician, and for the first time, took custody of his precocious young daughter.

Roosevelt played politics in a number of arenas, some successful, some not as much. Bringing his ideas of reform to bear, he became president of the board of the New York City Police Commissioners. While he was there, he earned much respect for his ideas. During his time as president of the board, he helped establish a bicycle squad, regular physical and mental exams for officers, standardized the use of pistols, created new disciplinary rules, and had telephones installed in the station houses.

Thanks to his fascination with Naval history and having written many books on the subject, he seemed to President William McKinley a perfect candidate for assistant secretary of the navy. Since the actual secretary of the navy did very little work, Roosevelt acted as though he was in charge as often as possible. In fact, ten days after the explosion of the USS Maine (the incident that sparked the Spanish-American War), Roosevelt waited until the secretary was out for a massage for four hours and declared himself acting secretary. He sent messages to the entire navy, telling them all to prepare for war, ordered ammunition and supplies to that end, and even asked for congressional permission to recruit sailors.

With the official declaration of war against Spain, Roosevelt resigned as the assistant secretary of the navy and created his own volunteer cavalry unit of cowboys from the West called "the Rough Riders." They went to Cuba and fought with distinction against the Spanish.

During the conflict, he rose to the rank of lieutenant colonel, and afterward insisted on being called colonel by all those who knew and interacted with him. He hated the nickname "Teddy," but the press loved it, and it proved quite popular.

In 1898, Roosevelt ran for governor of New York and won, but he had a significant problem with the political bosses in the state. Political bosses were people who headed large groups of people and told them who to vote for. They would do their best to control politicians by telling them that if they didn't do as they wished, they wouldn't get their votes. Roosevelt told them he'd let them give him advice and consent to appointments he made for positions in the state, but he twisted everything on its ear. Instead of letting them pick a candidate willy-nilly, Roosevelt would pick a small list of candidates he liked, who weren't corrupt and were right for the job. Then, he'd let the political bosses pick from those names.

To them, it was frustrating. It got even worse when Roosevelt kept pursuing a progressive agenda of things like better civil service laws, working to get teachers a minimum wage, and granting the state supreme court the power to inspect the financial transactions of private corporations. To say this upset the political bosses would be an understatement.

They looked far and wide for ways they could remove Roosevelt from office, but for all their political power, he was simply too popular. But the vice president had recently died, and there was a presidential election coming up, which gave them an idea. The position of vice president was one of much prestige and importance, but of little power. There wasn't much for a vice president to do in those days. He simply presided over the Senate and checked in occasionally to make sure the president was still alive. If they could get Roosevelt in that position, he'd have no power whatsoever over them, and he'd just go away.

Roosevelt himself wasn't keen on the idea of being vice president, knowing that it would limit his chance to reform anything. Roosevelt was also a man of modest means, and since the vice president was expected to host and attend many society functions, he had less than no interest.

But the political bosses still had their power over party politics, and Roosevelt's popularity in this case worked against him. He was the only popular candidate for vice president, well liked among everyone except the corporations and political bosses, and President McKinley kept quiet on the matter entirely. At the Republican Convention in June of 1900, Theodore Roosevelt was the presumptive vice presidential nominee, and there wasn't much he could do about it.

Once the job was forced on him, though, he tackled it with the full strength of his spirit. The Republicans decided to send Roosevelt on the road, debating William Jennings Bryan and making public appearances everywhere, while President McKinley greeted potential voters and influential people at the White House. Roosevelt was up to the rigors of the campaign, proclaiming himself "as strong as a bull moose."

Thanks to Roosevelt's vigorous campaigning and engaging personality, the McKinley-Roosevelt ticket was a foregone conclusion. After the election, Roosevelt did his best in the job, but found that he was very poor at it, even remarking that he was the "poorest presiding officer the Senate ever had."

This gave him plenty of time to spend with his second wife and the six children they had together.

He expected the next four years to continue this way, until he received a message in September of 1901. President McKinley had been shot, and Theodore was needed in Buffalo, New York immediately.

When he arrived, it would seem the president was going to recover, so Roosevelt left for a trip to the Adirondack Mountains. On September 13th, a Park Ranger found Roosevelt and told him that he'd received a message from the secretary of war and that the situation had changed. He was once more needed in Buffalo immediately. Roosevelt left instantly, only to find that the president had already passed away by the time he reached Buffalo.

On September 14th, at 42 years of age, Theodore Roosevelt was sworn in as the youngest man ever to become president.

As president, he kept McKinley's advisors and cabinet and vowed to continue shepherding McKinley's policies. It wasn't long before his own policies found their way into his work, though. One of his first notable acts as president was to deliver a State of the Union address that vehemently attacked corporations (which he called "trusts") and made a compelling case for their regulation. He said of the corporations that "...there are real and grave evils, one of the chief being overcapitalization because of its many baleful consequences; and a resolute and practical effort must be made to correct these evils... There is a widespread conviction in the minds of the American people that the great corporations known as trusts are in certain of their features and tendencies hurtful to the general welfare... It is based upon sincere conviction that combination and concentration should be, not prohibited, but supervised and within reasonable limits controlled; and in my judgment this conviction is right."

Roosevelt was a great progressive, working hard to balance the rights and needs of the average American against the desires of freedom on the parts of corporations. In one instance, he even intervened on behalf of workers in strikes, helping them get better pay for shorter hours and getting the company once again producing goods and making money.

During his time in the White House, President Roosevelt inadvertently allowed a disruptive gang to wreak havoc. The "White House Gang," as they were called, would arrive on the scene, shooting spitballs at portraits and playing pranks, and that caught the attention of the press. The leader of this gang? Quentin Roosevelt, the president's youngest son. His playmates were school friends and the children of those who worked in the White House and were near his same age. The boys made no discriminations based on race, color, creed, or even age. They even admitted the president himself into their gang.

Theodore Roosevelt served as president with distinction until 1909. During his time in office, he did much to aid in the well-being of Americans everywhere. He signed into law things like the Meat Inspection Act of 1906 and the Pure Food and Drug Act. Conservation was another issue very important to him. While in office, he created the U.S. Forest Service, 150 national forests, 5 national parks, and 18 national monuments. Thanks to his foresight, President Roosevelt protected more than 230,000,000 acres of public land that we can enjoy today.

In 1908, he chose not to run for another term in office and hand-picked his successor in William Taft.

Taft won the election, and as soon as he took office, Roosevelt went on a safari across Africa. He went to hunt for specimens that could be placed in the Smithsonian and the Natural History Museum in New York. During the safari, Roosevelt and his hunting party captured more than 11,000 animals, ranging in size from insects to hippopotamuses and elephants. Roosevelt shipped so many animals and specimens to the Smithsonian in the name of science that it took them years to mount and catalogue them all.

WILLIAM TAFT

He even wrote a book about his experiences called African Game Trails.

When Roosevelt returned from his travels, he found that Taft had proved inept at his job, angering and alienating constituents on all sides of every issue. Roosevelt was furious that he seemed to have abandoned the progressive legacy that swept him into office. Roosevelt saw himself as the only person who could save the Republican Party from Taft's destructive policies and incompetence, so he reentered the political arena to challenge Taft for the

Republican presidential nomination.

Things at the Republican Convention weren't going to be as easy for Roosevelt as he would have liked. After it became apparent that Taft would win renomination, Roosevelt and his supporters marched out of the convention and within hours had formed the Progressive Party. When a reporter asked Roosevelt if he was up to the challenge of another presidential campaign, he replied once more that he was "as fit as a bull moose." And thus the Progressive Party became the Bull Moose Party.

The election of 1912 was intense, with four major candidates running. For the first time in years the Democrats nominated someone other than William Jennings Bryan, instead fielding Woodrow Wilson as their candidate. The Republicans had Taft and Roosevelt was the nominee from the progressive Bull Moose Party. The fourth candidate was Eugene V. Debs, who ran on the Socialist Party ticket.

On October 14, 1912, Roosevelt was campaigning in Milwaukee, Wisconsin and was set to give a lengthy, 50-page speech to supporters when he was shot in the chest by a man named John Schrank.

JOHN SCHRANK

John Schrank was a saloon-keeper from New York who sold everything and began to drift aimlessly. Studying the Bible, he became very religious and would walk around the streets at night, causing no trouble whatsoever.

In papers found after the shooting, Schrank had written that the ghost of William McKinley came to him in a dream and begged the man to avenge his death, pointing to a portrait of Theodore Roosevelt.

In his personal life, Schrank had a problem with Roosevelt's desire to serve a third term. At that time, there were no limits on how many terms a president could serve, and Schrank felt the unspoken tradition of presidents to not seek third terms was sacred and inviolable. In his delusions and conviction, Schrank began to follow the president, from New Orleans up to Wisconsin where he made his move.

Roosevelt was eating dinner at the nearby Gilpatrick Hotel before his speech at the Milwaukee Auditorium. News reached Schrank that the former president was at the hotel, so he went there to perform his act.

The president, having finished his meal, was heading for his car to take him to the speech when Schrank acted, shooting Roosevelt once in the chest.

And there the bullet remained..

Schrank was quickly arrested and Roosevelt was tended to, but they found that the bullet had passed through the metal glasses case and the fifty page speech Roosevelt was to deliver before embedding into Roosevelt's chest.

Those around wanted Roosevelt to go immediately to the hospital, but since he wasn't coughing up blood (which clearly meant the bullet hadn't made it into his lungs), Roosevelt refused and instead decided he wanted to deliver the speech anyway. Against their better judgement, they drove Roosevelt to the Milwaukee Auditorium where he spoke, still bleeding, for ninety minutes.

He opened his speech, saying, "Friends, I shall ask you to be as quiet as possible. I don't know whether you fully understand that I have just been shot; but it takes more than that to kill a Bull Moose. But fortunately I had my manuscript, so you see I was going to make a long speech, and there is a bullet -- there is where the bullet went through -- and it probably saved me from it going into my heart. The bullet is in me now, so that I cannot make a very long speech, but I will try my best."

After the speech, Roosevelt finally made it to a doctor, where they determined they'd do more damage by trying to remove it than by just sewing him up. Roosevelt had the bullet lodged in the muscle of his chest for the rest of his life.

Schrank said later that he wasn't trying to kill Roosevelt himself, but "Roosevelt-the-third-termer." His intent was to send a message to any other president seeking a third term, and that McKinley is the one who told him the act must be performed. He was deemed insane and was remanded to the Central State Mental Hospital in Waupun, Wisconsin until the time of his death in 1943.

Wilson and Taft both suspended their campaigns for a week while Roosevelt convalesced, but the fight for the presidency then resumed. Wilson became the ultimate victor. Roosevelt placed second, Taft and Debs a distant third and fourth.

For the rest of his life, Roosevelt continued exploring the world and maintaining an interest in politics. He criticized Wilson's handling of World War I from the beginning. While Wilson advocated neutrality, Roosevelt insisted we help the Allies immediately.

Tragedy struck him in late 1918 when he heard word that his youngest, most beloved son, Quentin, was shot and killed during an aerial battle over the German countryside during the war. It was devastating to him, and those around him said he never quite recovered from that shock. After all, it was his influence that brought his son into the war.

Roosevelt himself passed away in 1919 in his sleep, at the age of sixty. The vice president at the time, Thomas Marshall, commented that, "Death had to take Roosevelt sleeping, for if he had been awake, there would have been a fight."

When told of Roosevelt's death, his would-be assassin expressed remorse at the former president's passing, conceding that he was a truly great American.

Scout's Presidential Portrait

Chapter 6

Franklin D. Roosevelt (1882-1945)

32nd President of the United States

    According to political historians, Franklin Roosevelt has been consistently ranked as one of the most successful and influential presidents the United States has ever had. He's the only president who served more than two terms in office (he was elected four times!), helped guide the country through the worst depression we'd ever known up to that time, and was the commander-in-chief during World War II.

FRANKLIN D. ROOSEVELT

While Franklin was at Harvard studying for his Bachelor of Arts degree, his fifth cousin, Theodore, became president of the United States. Because of his leadership skills and charisma, Theodore became Franklin's hero, and he sought to emulate him in every way on his road to become the president. He ran for the state Senate in New York (Theodore had served as an assembly-man), he became assistant secretary to the navy as Theodore had been, and, just like Teddy, he became governor of New York.

Long before he was our 32nd president, even before he was governor of New York, Franklin Roosevelt was vacationing with his family in Canada when he was stricken with an illness.

He was diagnosed with polio.

Polio (or poliomyelitis) is a disease that is sometimes known as infantile paralysis, because it usually affects children. Since the 1840s, polio had become a worldwide epidemic, and it robbed many hundreds of thousands of people their ability to walk, because it weakened and ate at the muscles in the spinal column and legs. Though the paralysis from polio was permanent, Franklin refused to believe it. He tried every form of therapy he could think of to overcome his paralysis, but the only thing that worked was his own inner strength. He "walked" with the aid of a cane and one of his sons holding up his other side. He convinced many people that he could still walk, albeit with great difficulty.

While convincing the world he could walk publicly, privately he spent much of his time in a wheelchair that he designed himself. He didn't let his paralysis get in the way of his career or his life. He drove a car with specially created hand-operated controls, and he made sure the public never knew he was paralyzed, afraid they'd never elect a leader who couldn't walk.

In fact, only two photographs exist of Franklin Roosevelt in his wheelchair, and only four seconds of film footage exist of his "walking" with the aid of his cane and his son.

But his illness never stopped him.

When Franklin Roosevelt began his first run for president, things were not going well in America. After the big stock market crash in 1929, money became far less valuable, unemployment skyrocketed, and no one had any money to buy products. Supply and demand was completely broken. We were also in the midst of prohibition, so some of the wealthiest people were mob-sters and bootleggers who provided alcohol and liquor to people looking for a drink. Prohibition was the period of time where alcoholic drinks like beer and wine were completely outlawed in the United States, as outlined in the

Eighteenth Amendment to the Constitution.

The president at the time, Herbert Hoover, did little to stop the problem and Roosevelt campaigned on the promise of a "New Deal" for Americans. He wanted to get the American people back to work and end the suffering they'd endured because of the Depression, but he wasn't exactly sure how to do it.

Herbert Hoover, the 31st president, did very little to manage the Depression and was seen as a do-nothing during the election, claiming gloom and doom for the problem. Roosevelt, on the other hand, maintained a positive attitude and promised things would get better for those hit hardest by the economic crash.

The voters felt like Roosevelt would do better to handle the Great Depression and so, in November of 1932, he was elected to be the 32nd president of the United States. Back then, the new president wasn't inaugurated until March, leaving the outgoing president almost half a year to wrap up his business (from November to March). After the election, President Hoover did very little to fix the crisis and Roosevelt toured the country giving speeches and meeting with Americans, finding out from them how best to fix things.

It was at an impromptu speech in Miami, Florida during the president-elect's travels, that a man tried to kill him.

GIUSEPPE ZANGARA

Giuseppe Zangara was born in Italy and served in the Italian Army during World War I. In 1923, he immigrated to the United States with his uncle. He was a working class citizen; a brick layer with a poor education. He had a hard time finding work and blamed President Hoover for his handling of the Depression. As soon as Franklin Roosevelt won the election, he turned his anger toward the incoming president.

Zangara was what they called in those days an "anarchist." He hated the government and disliked a system that allowed some men to be so rich while others could be so poor. When he heard that the president-to-be was going to be giving a speech alongside Anton Cermak, the mayor of Chicago, he bought a .32 calibre pistol and attended the speech with the intent to kill Roosevelt.

Roosevelt gave his speech and greeted the crowd from the back seat of his car while talking to the mayor next to him. That was when Zangara tried to make his move.

Fortunately, the would-be assassin was very short. At barely five feet tall, he couldn't see over the crowd to shoot his target. Zangara balanced himself precariously on an unstable, wooden folding chair, and from 10 feet away and over the heads of the crowd, he blindly fired at Franklin Roosevelt. He fired at least five bullets before he was wrestled to the ground by the crowd.

Four members of the public were injured by his shooting spree, and a bullet hit the Chicago mayor in the stomach, but the one person who made it through without a scratch was Franklin Roosevelt.

The crowd handled Zangara until the police could arrive, and the president-elect's car raced Cermak to the hospital. Roosevelt tried comforting the wounded man on the way, but the mayor was steadfast. "I'm glad it was me," he told Roosevelt, "and not you, Mr. President."

Zangara was put to trial almost immediately, but he hadn't actually killed anyone at that point. It took 19 days for Mayor Cermak to die of his wound to the gut. After that, Zangara was finally charged with murder and sentenced to die in the electric chair. When the judge asked him why he tried to kill Roosevelt, Zangara, in his very broken English said, "I got it in my mind capitalist hurt people. They are to blame for my stomach hurting. My stomach was hurting bad. It was like I was on fire. It burns my mind, I act like a drunken man. It came in my mind when I was suffering."

Though some think a possibility exists that Zangara was trying to kill Cermak the whole time, others think Zangara was probably just a hurt and confused man who didn't know what he was doing.

Franklin Roosevelt was sworn into office in March of 1933, and because of his policies of relief, recovery, and reform, the president cut the unemployment rate almost in half by the end of his first term.

Through his career as president, before the start of World War II, he helped enact social programs that helped us take care of the hungry, the sick, the poor, and the elderly, and helped reshape our country into what he referred to as the "Great Society."

Through World War II, he led America through one of its most difficult and trying times, fighting the global threat of the Third Reich and Adolf Hitler. He helped save the country and the world from ruin, and he did so without the use of his legs, serving as an example of what the American spirit is truly capable of.

Scout's Presidential Portrait

Chapter 7

Harry S. Truman (1884-1972)

33rd President of the United States

Born to simple Scots-Irish farmers in Missouri, Harry S. Truman prospered himself as a farmer before joining the Missouri National Guard.

Truman wore glasses and had terrible vision, which would have ordinarily kept him out of service, but he memorized the eye chart, and they were none the wiser. Eventually, they sent him to France during World War I, where he served as an artilleryman. By the end of his service and after the end of the war, Truman had risen to the rank of colonel. He was a feisty officer, keeping his artillery squad together during the roughest of times. At the end of the war, on November 11, 1918, his group was one of the last to fire shots in World War I. They shelled Germany after the signing of the Armistice, but before the ceasefire at 11 a.m. took effect.

In a statement that seemed at odds with his folksy persona, Truman said of his disappointment with the ceasefire, "It is a shame we can't go in and devastate Germany and cut off a few of the Dutch kids' hands and feet and scalp a few of their old men."

After returning home, Truman, who did not have a college degree (and is the last man to obtain the office of president without one), opened up a haberdashery and married his girlfriend, Bess Wallace.

After a few years of success with the hat-making shop, disaster struck the economy in 1921 and Truman's store went bankrupt. He struggled until 1934 to pay back all the debts.

It was during this period he decided to enter politics, gaining a judgeship; then in 1934 he was elected to the United States Senate as the senator from Missouri.

While in the Senate, Truman's greatest victory came during World War II with "the Truman Committee." Then-Senator Truman established a committee to fight waste and mismanagement in the war effort, eventually saving the government an estimated $15 billion dollars and thousands of lives.

This earned him the attention of the world.

At the same time, it was clear that President Roosevelt's health was deteriorating and political machines in the background knew that whoever was chosen as the new vice president during Roosevelt's 1944 campaign would most likely become the next president of the United States by default. Roosevelt's vice president at the time was a man named Henry A. Wallace, and the political machine that supported Roosevelt felt he might be too liberal to govern the way they wanted.

There were a few options available, but President Roosevelt decided he wanted Harry S. Truman, even though Truman didn't particularly want the job.

After a daring ruse set up by the president, Truman eventually accepted the job and campaigned with the president for his fourth term. The ruse was this: Roosevelt had set up a phone call that Truman was allowed to listen in on where Roosevelt asked political bosses whether Truman would be his vice president or not. When they told him he wouldn't, he made a show of getting very angry and telling them that Truman was disrupting party unity in the middle of the war and hung up angrily.

The entire call had been rehearsed before hand.

After that, how could he refuse?

The Roosevelt-Truman ticket beat Thomas Dewey and John Bricker with a 432-99 win in the electoral vote during the 1944 presidential election.

On January 20, 1945, Truman was sworn in as the vice president of the United States, alongside President Roosevelt for his fourth term. He had little contact with the president and was given no briefings about the war or anything else. The only way to describe his time as vice president was uneventful.

On April 12, 1945, in his twelfth year as president, Franklin Roosevelt died of a massive cerebral hemorrhage (a stroke) in Warm Springs, Georgia. After a long day presiding over the Senate, and only a few months on the job as vice president, Truman was called in by an urgent message to the White House. He assumed that the president wanted to meet him about an urgent matter, instead he was met by Mrs. Roosevelt and told that the president had passed away.

He was instantly concerned for the first lady who had just lost her husband, "Is there anything I can do for you?" he asked her.

To which she replied, "Is there anything we can do for you? You're the one in trouble now."

Suddenly sworn in as president after only 82 days in the number two position, Truman had to be quickly brought up to speed so that he could win the war still raging in both Europe and the Pacific. It was then that he was told of the top secret Manhattan Project and the existence of the atomic bomb.

Less than a month after taking office, the war in Europe was over after Germany's unconditional surrender, but Japan still held out on the Pacific front, refusing to give up.

With the Japanese holding strong and assuring the world that they wouldn't surrender, President Truman felt the best course of action was to use an atom bomb against them. In August, after being given another chance to surrender after the Potsdam Conference, the president authorized the nuclear attack against Japan.

On August 6, 1945, the United States dropped an atomic bomb named "Little Boy" on the city of Hiroshima, Japan, killing as many as 140,000 people. Two days later, another bomb, this one named "Fat Man," was dropped on Nagasaki, Japan, killing another 80,000 people.

After such total devastation to two of their cities, Japan surrendered unconditionally on August 14, 1945, ending World War II.

In 1948, Harry S. Truman narrowly won reelection. In fact, in one of the most famous blunders in newspaper history, the media called the election in favor of Thomas Dewey on Election Day, only to find out by morning their headline declaring Truman's defeat was inaccurate.

He spent his time fighting members of the opposition party on his Fair Deal plan and enjoying their support on foreign issues. During this time, the White House underwent a renovation, and President Truman relocated his residence to the nearby Blair House.

Meanwhile, trouble was brewing in the territory of Puerto Rico. Puerto Rico had become a territory of the United States at the conclusion of the Spanish-American War with the Treaty of Paris of 1898. In 1917, Puerto Ricans were made full U.S. citizens, granting them the ability to fight during World War I. This granted them the full protections of the United States Constitution, and they would be governed by the federal laws of the United States and use our system of money.

During the 1940s, there was a resurgence of Puerto Rican nationalism and certain factions of the population wanted the United States to leave them with their own sovereign independence, but some didn't like that idea. In 1948, a bill (called Law 53) was introduced in the Puerto Rican Senate that would criminalize the display of a Puerto Rican flag. Law 53 made it a crime to speak out against the United States and in favor of Puerto Rican independence.

Some contested that Law 53 was unconstitutional because it limited the freedom of speech of American citizens, but others were, understandably, much more upset about it. Because of this law, hundreds were imprisoned and the Nationalists began to plot an armed revolution to overturn this infringement on their rights. The revolution was to have happened in 1952, but after a series of arrests of Nationalist leaders in 1950, uprisings and revolts happened much earlier than planned. In the town of Jayuya, Nationalists took over the town, killing police officers, burning down the post office, and raising the Puerto Rican flag in the town square, proclaiming Puerto Rico a free state.

In response, the United States declared martial law (meaning a complete military take over, suspending rights and freedoms) and attacked Jayuya with bombers, artillery, and assorted infantry. The battle lasted for three days, and the Nationalists couldn't compete with the military might of the United States.

OSCAR COLLAZO   GRISELIO TORRESOLA

When news of this reached Nationalists Oscar Collazo and Griselio Tor-resola, on October 30, 1950, they made the decision to assassinate President Truman. These two friends met in New York City and were deeply invest-ed in Puerto Rican independence. They had relatives that were wounded in the massacres and were aghast that the news was being under-reported and downplayed by the American media. By assassinating President Truman, they knew they'd be committing suicide, but felt they would bring the attention to Puerto Rican independence that it deserved.

Over the next two days, Collazo and Torresola trained with firearms and staked out the Blair House. On Halloween, after saying fond goodbyes to their families, they bought one-way train tickets to Washington, D.C. and checked into a hotel. They took a taxicab to the Blair House and found two guard shacks right on the sidewalk in front of a townhouse. The front door was used by the president and his guests.

They left, ate lunch, and returned.

At about 2:20 in the afternoon of November 1, 1950, about a half an hour before the president was scheduled to unveil a statue at Arlington National Cemetery, Collazo and Torresola returned to murder President Truman.

So much happened over the course of that next half a minute that it's hard to determine what really happened. President Truman was, indeed, at home. Two of the guards, Secret Service Agent Floyd Boring and Private Leslie Coffelt, were chatting on the sidewalk outside of Private Joseph Davidson's guard booth. Donald Birdzell was on the outside of the front door, while Stewart Stout stood just inside the front door, guarding the stairwell, within arms reach of a machine gun.

In order to get to Truman, Collazo and Torresola had to get through all of these armed guards and into the house. Things began when Collazo pulled out his Walther P38 handgun, quietly came behind Birdzell, and pulled the trigger.

Fortunately for Birdzell, Collazo hadn't chambered a round and so the gun didn't go off at all. Birdzell whipped around at the sound of the click, smashing the gun away with his fist. Collazo was finally able to get a bullet in the chamber and managed to shoot Birdzell in the knee.

Wanting to lead the shooting away from the house, Birdzell limped into the street and opened fire on Collazo, while the others readied their weapons to join in the firefight.

Using this as a distraction, Torresola approached Private Coffelt's guard box and shot him three times: in his chest, his stomach, and his legs. Downs, who was readying his machine gun from the door, was Torresola's next target, and he was shot three times as well. Then, Torresola turned to Birdzell who was still shooting at his partner. He disabled him by shooting his other knee out.

At this point, there was nothing to stop Torresola and Collazo from entering the door and proceeding to kill President Truman.

Except that with his final act, while struggling to remain conscious, Private Coffelt raised his pistol and shot Torresola through the head with one shot. Then he passed out.

With Torresola dead and Collazo shot in the chest, the battle was over.

As the shooting ended, Truman raced to the window to see what was going on, but was quickly pulled back for fear there might be more accomplices in the crowd.

LESLIE COFFELT

Coffelt was raced to the hospital and died four hours later. His heroic action, with the last of his consciousness, is largely believed to have been what saved the president's life. Coffelt's wife was asked by the administration to visit Puerto Rico and heal the wounds with the United States.

Collazo was put to trial in 1951 and sentenced to death after an unsuccessful plea of insanity against the advice of his lawyers. The execution was to take place August 1, 1952, but President Truman commuted the sentence to life in prison, not wanting to make a martyr out of Collazo for his cause.

In 1979, President Jimmy Carter commuted the sentence entirely for the now-elderly Collazo, who lived quietly in Puerto Rico for the rest of his days until his death in 1994.

In May of 1952, President Truman dedicated a plaque in front of the Blair House to Private Leslie Coffelt, in honor of the sacrifice he made. Truman vowed to cooperate with his guards in every way he could. He had a renewed respect for those who protect the president and took it upon himself to be more aware of the responsibility he had to them.

Scout's Presidential Portrait

Chapter 8

John F. Kennedy (1917-1963)

35th President of the United States

At 43 years old in 1960, John Fitzgerald Kennedy was the youngest man ever to be elected president of the United States. Born into a wealthy Massachusetts family, he attended private schools through most of his life and gravitated toward the water for his hobbies. He was an avid sailor and was on the varsity swim team at Harvard College. He graduated in 1940 from Harvard with a Bachelor of Science cum laude (which means "with honor") in International Affairs. His thesis was about British appeasement prior to World War II, and it was turned into a bestselling book called Why England Slept.

Kennedy tried joining the army prior to American involvement in the Second World War, and was disqualified due to chronic back pain, but the navy took him. He served as an ensign in the office of the secretary of the navy when Pearl Harbor was attacked on December 7, 1941. Eventually,

Kennedy was trained as an officer and was given command of PT-109. The PT in PT-109 stood for Patrol Torpedo, and Kennedy and his crew were tasked with patrolling parts of the Pacific Ocean, ever on the lookout for Japanese boats that would attack American troops.

In August of 1943, Kennedy's PT boat and 14 others were sent to intercept five Japanese destroyers that were supposed to be running near the southern tip of Kolombangara Island. When they found the destroyers, the PT captains launched as many as 60 torpedoes in that direction; they scored few hits, but did scare the destroyers away. Most of the PT boats were recalled to the base, but PT-109 was ordered to stay and patrol in case the destroyers returned.

Running as quietly as possible to avoid detection, PT-109 moved slowly through the moonless night in search of targets alongside two other PT boats. Soon, the crew of PT-109 noticed that they were in the direct path of the Japanese destroyer Amagiri, which was traveling at a very high speed. They had only 10 seconds to react, but it was all for naught. The Amagiri cut Kennedy's PT boat in two. Two crew members were killed outright, and two more were wounded badly. With half the ship sinking and the other half on fire, the remaining crew had to make a decision.

Kennedy gathered them all up in the water and asked them if they would fight or surrender. One account reported that Kennedy said, "There's nothing in the book about a situation like this. A lot of you men have families, and some of you have children. What do you want to do? I have nothing to lose."

The men opted to fight, and so they chose a small, deserted island free of Japanese troops about three and a half miles away called Plum Pudding Island and began to swim. Kennedy, even with his bad back, swam the whole way there himself, towing one of his wounded crewman by the lifejacket with his teeth.

The other two PT boats on patrol with PT-109 tried firing torpedoes, but they either missed or misfired completely, fleeing the scene and returning to base without looking for survivors.

It took Kennedy and his men four hours to reach the island, which they did without being assaulted by sharks or crocodiles, which were common in those waters. Plum Pudding Island was only about 100 yards around and had no food or water. While the crew hid from sight of passing Japanese barges, Kennedy swam another three miles to two other islands until he found Olasana Island, which had fresh water and coconuts.

Fortunately for Kennedy, the explosion of PT-109 didn't go completely unnoticed. An Australian coast watcher who manned a secret Allied observation tower atop the volcano on the Japanese-held Kolombangara Island saw the explosion and dispatched two native scouts in small canoes to search the area of the explosion and the surrounding islands.

It was six days before Kennedy and his men were spotted by the scouts who initially took them for enemies. It took some convincing before the scouts believed that Kennedy and his men were allies, but there were 11 survivors, and they couldn't all fit in the canoe. The scout suggested that Kennedy carve a message into a coconut that he could canoe back to Allied forces.

Eventually, the message was delivered after the scouts canoed through 35 miles of waters patrolled heavily by Japanese forces. Another PT boat was able to make it in and rescue the survivors.

Kennedy was given awards and honors for his actions, and the coconut shell with the message carved into it was encased in glass, sat on the president's desk during his time in office, and is still on display at the John F. Kennedy Library in Boston, Massachusetts.

The eventual president would find other duties during the war until his honorable discharge in 1945, before the Japanese surrender.

After a brief stint working in newspapers for William Randolph Hearst, Kennedy was elected to the Massachusetts 11th congressional district and served as a congressman from his home state for the next six years. Then, in 1952, he won his election to become a senator from Massachusetts. After a term and a half in the United States Senate, John F. Kennedy decided it was time for him to run for president of the United States. On July 13, after a close primary, the Democratic National Convention nominated John F. Ken-

nedy to be their candidate, and he asked his single strongest primary chal-
lenger, Lyndon B. Johnson, to be his vice presidential running mate.

The Republicans nominated Richard M. Nixon to be their candidate,
and the two participated in the first televised presidential debates the United
States had ever seen. It was the first time television played a major role in
American politics, and it is seen by many as the thing that helped Kennedy
win the general election. In the debates, he looked much more calm and col-
lected than his opponent, and he was much better suited for live television.

The election was close, but Kennedy took home 303 electoral votes compared to Nixon's 219.

At noon on January 20, 1961, John F. Kennedy was sworn in as the 35th president of the United States.

Because of the Cold War raging between the United States and the Soviet Union, much of Kennedy's accomplishments as president reflect his handling of that crisis. One event in particular, the Cuban Missile Crisis, tested Kennedy more than almost any other president had ever been forced to endure. The Russians were deploying nuclear missiles on the island of Cuba, just off the coast of Florida. It was not something the United States could allow, and it caused a standoff that some say was the closest we've ever come to the breakout of World War III.

At the end of his inaugural address, John F. Kennedy said to his fellow Americans, "Ask not what your country can do for you--ask what you can do for your country. My fellow citizens of the world: ask not what America will do for you, but what together we can do for the freedom of man." With that sentiment in mind, one of Kennedy's most important and lasting contributions came in the guise of the formation of the Peace Corps. Through the Peace Corps, Americans could volunteer to help less fortunate nations develop better education, farming, healthcare, and many other things. Since its formation in 1961, hundreds of thousands have volunteered with the Peace Corps and have done their part to make the world a better place.

Kennedy was also a vocal supporter of the Civil Rights movement, and he even signed an executive order that created the Presidential Commission on the Status of Women, led by Eleanor Roosevelt.

Perhaps the single largest kept promise of John F. Kennedy's was our race to land a man on the moon before the end of the 1960s. Before his death, he shepherded the legislation and budget that kept the National Aeronautics and Space Administration (NASA) working on a moon landing that would put us on the lunar surface in 1969.

In November of 1963, President Kennedy made a trip to Dallas, Texas in an effort to smooth out political differences between the Democratic Party and the conservative governor of Texas, John Connally.

The trip was made, and on November 22, 1963, Air Force One landed at Dallas Love Field. There, President Kennedy and his wife, Jacqueline, were met by Governor Connally and his wife. They got into an open-air limousine and began the motorcade along a 10 mile parade route that would end in a luncheon at the Dallas Trade Mart.

President Kennedy never made it.

The man who would end President Kennedy's life was named Lee Harvey Oswald. In 1956, just after his 17th birthday, Oswald joined the United States Marines, which trained him as a radar operator. In his rifle training, he was qualified as a sharpshooter by the Marines. In 1959, he was discharged from the Marines after claiming his mother needed him to care for her, but then he traveled to the Soviet Union in an attempt to defect. He tried unsuc-cessfully to renounce his American citizenship, stayed in the country long enough to meet and marry a 19 year old student named Marina Prusakova. After their first child was born in February of 1962, they applied to return to the United States. In June, the Oswald family was allowed to come back to America, where they settled in the Dallas/Fort Worth area.

He purchased a rifle and tried to assassinate a retired general who was a notorious opponent of communism, a segregationist, and an outspoken mem-ber of the right wing fringe group, the John Birch Society. Oswald buried the rifle after the failed attempt.

After traveling around, doing odd jobs and promoting communist caus-es, Oswald returned to Dallas. When he got home, he was told about a job opening at the Texas School Book Depository by a neighbor and he was hired there on October 16, 1963. In the days leading up to the president's visit, the newspapers repeatedly printed information about the parade route he would take, right past the Book Depository.

We'll never know for sure why Lee Harvey Oswald decided to shoot Pres-ident Kennedy, but we do know the facts of what happened.

At 11:40 in the morning, President Kennedy and his wife got off of Air Force One and got into the back seat of the uncovered limousine that would take them to their destination. Governor Connally and his wife took the front seat.

Since the route had been so widely publicized, throngs of supporters (and surely some detractors) lined the streets to wave to the president.

The first lady of Texas turned back to the president, who was seated directly behind her, and said of the crowds, "Mr. President, you can't say Dal-las doesn't love you."

One onlooker at Dealey Plaza, Abraham Zapruder, managed to catch everything that happened next on 8mm film.

At approximately 12:30 p.m. on November 22, 1963, Lee Harvey Oswald, from a window on the sixth floor of the Texas School Book Depository, opened fire on the presidential motorcade as it passed through Dealey Plaza.

One of the shots entered the president's upper back, penetrated his neck, and damaged his spine and right lung. Another shot hit President Kennedy directly in the head, just as he passed Abraham Zapruder's vantage point, forever burning that moment on film. After the president had been shot, Mrs. Kennedy crawled onto the back of the car; some said it was to retrieve a piece of the president's skull.

The limousine went straight to Parkland Memorial Hospital, where doctors went to work both on the president, and on Governor Connally, who had also been shot.

After firing his sniper shots, Lee Harvey Oswald fled the Texas School Book Depository. After making his way to the boarding house he stayed in to change clothes, Oswald was stopped on the street by a police officer named J.D. Tippit, who spoke to him. Oswald shot him four times, killing him. In a rush, Oswald ducked into a shoe store. Suspicions aroused, the manager of the shoe store watched Oswald continue down the street and sneak into a movie at the Texas Theatre without paying.

The shoe store manager alerted the theatre's usher, who promptly called the police.

When the police arrived and the house lights went up, Oswald stood, saying, "Well, it's all over now," just before pulling a pistol from the front of his pants. He tried firing at an officer, but was disarmed after a struggle.

By 2 p.m., just an hour and a half after the president had been shot, Lee Harvey Oswald was in police custody.

While the police were apprehending the assassin, doctors at the hospital were working hard to save the life of President Kennedy. But it was no good; there was nothing they could do. At 1 p.m., after a priest had administered the last rights and his heart stopped, the doctors declared the president dead.

At the same time Lee Harvey Oswald was being booked in the police station, President Kennedy was put in a casket and brought out to Love Field and placed aboard Air Force One.

At 2:38 p.m., aboard Air Force One, with a shocked, blood-soaked Jacqueline Kennedy at his side, Lyndon B. Johnson was sworn in as the 36th president of the United States.

For two days, while he was being held in the Dallas police station, Oswald was interrogated thoroughly. He denied killing the president, he denied owning a rifle, he denied anything that could connect him to the assassination.

After learning nothing from an uncooperative Oswald, the Dallas police were forced to transfer their prisoner to the county jail so he could be brought up on charges. As he was being led through the basement of the police headquarters, a Dallas night club owner named Jack Ruby appeared from the mob, stepped up to Oswald and the police, and shot the president's assassin. Oswald was raced to the same hospital that received the president and the Texas governor, and died there 48 hours and 7 minutes after the president himself was pronounced dead.

With his death, he took with him any certainty of his motive.

For Jack Ruby, Kennedy's assassin's assassin, he claimed he did it as a spur of the moment decision to save Mrs. Kennedy from the grief of a prolonged trial. Ruby was sentenced to death, but that was commuted to a prison stay. He died in 1967 of a pulmonary embolism (blockage of the lungs) in the same hospital in which President Kennedy and Lee Harvey Oswald were pronounced dead.

Over the years, persistent claims of conspiracy have been called, and people have said that it was impossible that Lee Harvey Oswald could have acted alone. To put these rumors to rest, President Johnson employed the chief justice of the Supreme Court, Earl Warren, to head a commission to collect all of the evidence and declare once and for all that Lee Harvey Oswald acted alone.

President Kennedy's casket was brought to the White House for 24 hours, and then was brought to the capitol building to lie in state. On Monday, November 25, 1963, President Kennedy was laid to rest in Arlington National Cemetery. After the burial, Mrs. Kennedy lit an eternal flame that still burns today in honor of her husband, the fallen president.

This was truly a national tragedy, and the country was in a state of shock. President Johnson declared the 25th to be a national day of mourning.

Over the next three years alone, it was estimated that 16 million people had visited the president's grave. By 1971, an additional 7 million people came to pay their respects.

At 43, John F. Kennedy was the youngest man elected president. At 46, he was also the youngest to die.

Scout's Presidential Portrait

Scout's Assassination Interpretation

Chapter 9

Richard Nixon (1913-1994)

37th President of the United States

Richard Milhous Nixon was born in Yorba Linda, California, and he was raised by conservative parents as a Quaker. His family was poor, and he worked at his father's grocery store. He did well enough in his classes to receive a full scholarship to Duke University School of Law. In 1937, he graduated third in his class, keeping his scholarship the entire time.

After practicing law for a time and working in government, he joined the navy in 1942 to fight in World War II. He went to Officers Candidate School and was commissioned as an ensign, eventually working his way up to lieutenant commander at which time he resigned his commission on New Year's Day, 1946. He oversaw logistics and saw no actual combat during the course of the war.

When he came back, he entered the public sector. He spent 1946 campaigning for California's 12th congressional district seat in the House of Representatives, eventually winning handily.

During his time in Congress, Nixon was a member of the House Un-American Activities Committee. The committee was established to root out threats to America and narrowed its focus for a time on rooting out communism as though it was a bad word. In 1947, they held hearings that investigated the influence of Hollywood films as a means of communist propaganda. Many producers, actors, and directors refused to cooperate or name names of friends and colleagues that were suspected of having sympathies with communist ideals.

Nixon found fame on the committee when he broke the Alger Hiss story. Hiss was a member of the State Department and had been a Soviet spy.

In 1950, Nixon ran for the position of the senator of California and won.

He wasn't a senator for long when General Dwight D. Eisenhower, a hero of World War II, chose him as his running mate for the presidential election. Richard Nixon could be called the first modern vice president, because he actually took on responsibility from the office of the president and didn't just wait to see if the president was in danger of passing away.

After a handy reelection, Vice President Nixon worked hard to shepherd the Civil Rights Act of 1957 through the Senate, and he convinced President Eisenhower to sign it. The goal of that act was to ensure that all Americans could exercise their right to vote. It was a significant step on the long road toward equal rights for all.

As vice president (and long after his own presidency), Nixon was an affable statesman. President Eisenhower even sent him to the Soviet Union in 1959 for an event in Moscow. While on a tour with Soviet Premier Nikita Khrushchev, Nixon engaged him in a friendly debate about capitalism and communism.

The next year, Richard Nixon ran for the office of the president against John F. Kennedy and lost narrowly. He kept his hat out of the ring for the 1964 election, instead supporting Barry Goldwater, who lost to Lyndon Johnson. By 1968, he was ready to run for office again, this time against a Democrat named Hubert Humphrey.

Due in some part to public distaste with the Vietnam War, which Nixon promised to end, and the inclusion of third party candidate George Wallace, Nixon narrowly won the office and was sworn in as president on January 20, 1969. During Nixon's first term, he made great strides in foreign policy, bringing the United States and China closer together than ever before since the formation of the People's Republic of China.

True to his word, Richard Nixon ended the war in Vietnam by 1973 and eliminated the draft, meaning that only people who signed up to serve in the armed forces would do so.

In one of his most lasting positive legacies, Richard Nixon created the Environmental Protection Agency, tasking them with safe-guarding our country's natural resources. He also presided over the Clean Air Act and helped established OSHA (the Occupational Safety and Health Administration).

President Nixon is perhaps best known, however, for the Watergate scandal. The Watergate scandal encompasses all of the shady activities Nixon condoned and often ordered on his behalf in order to win reelection in 1972. He used government agencies to harass and spy on political opponents. The entire thing was made public by Washington Post reporters Bob Woodward and Carl Bernstein, after a group of men were caught breaking into the headquarters of the Democratic National Committee at the Watergate hotel in Washington, D.C. With the help of their secret information source, Deep Throat, they were able to tie the burglaries all the way to the Oval Office.

SAMUEL BYCK

While they were uncovering their investigation, however, there was a disturbed man on the loose. Samuel Byck was an unemployed man with nothing to lose. He suffered from severe depression and began to believe that the government was a massive conspiracy to oppress the poor and working class.

In 1972, he sent letters to all kinds of government officials and others (including Jonas Salk, the scientist who cured polio, and the famous composer Leonard Bernstein) threatening them. One of the letters went to President Nixon. The Secret Service investigated Byck briefly, but decided he was harmless.

Two years passed, and in 1974, Byck decided he was going to kill President Nixon for real this time.

Knowing the Secret Service was already aware of him and would try to stop him if he tried to buy a gun, Byck stole a .22 caliber gun from a friend and then made bomb out of jugs of gasoline. All the while, he was making audio recordings of his plot so people would understand he was a hero after the assassination.

Byck decided it would be too difficult to get close enough to the president to shoot him, so his best course of action was to hijack a 747 and crash it into the White House.

On February 22, 1974, Samuel Byck drove out to Baltimore/Washington International Airport where he shot and killed an airport police officer, then stormed the tarmac. There, he boarded Delta Airlines Flight 523 to Atlanta with a gun and a suitcase containing his homemade bomb.

Once on board, Byck told the pilots to get the plane in the air. When they stalled, explaining that they couldn't take off until the wheel blocks were removed, he shot them both, killing one and wounding the other, then grabbed a random passenger. He put a gun to her head and told her to "fly the plane."

Byck then turned to a flight attendant and demanded she close the door or he would blow up the plane. At the same time, the police responding to the crisis tried shooting out the tires of the plane so it couldn't take off, but their .38 bullets simply bounced off the tires.

When it was clear Byck wasn't backing down, one officer stormed the plane, shooting four bullets, trying to shoot Byck through the door. Byck was wounded, but the door was still closed. Before authorities were able to get into the plane, a wounded Byck shot himself in the head, ending his own life.

That was as close as he ever got to killing President Nixon, but it was close enough. From then on, the Secret Service established methods of taking down an airplane for their rooftop observation teams.

As for Nixon himself, he would end up resigning in disgrace for his part in the Watergate scandal on August 9, 1974. To date, Nixon was the only person in the history of the United States to resign the office of president.

Scout's Presidential Portrait

Chapter 10

Gerald Ford (1913-2006)

38th President of the United States

Gerald Ford was born Leslie Lynch King, Jr. in Nebraska in 1913. His natural father was abusive and because of this, his parents separated just sixteen days after he was born. In an effort to get completely away, the future president's mother moved him to Grand Rapids, Michigan to live with her parents. After two and a half years there, she married a man named Gerald Rudolff Ford and decided to change her son's name to Gerald Rudolph Ford, Jr.

He lived completely unaware of his birth father until he was 17 years old, when one day, while waiting tables in a restaurant, Leslie King, Sr. arrived unexpectedly and told him the truth. But it wasn't the end of the world. Ford loved his mother and stepfather, and his true lineage never hindered him.

Gerald Ford is the only president who has achieved the rank of Eagle Scout in the Boy Scouts of America.

Ford was an all-star high school football player, and went on to lead the Wolverines from the University of Michigan to two undefeated seasons in 1932 and 1933. The future president graduated in 1935 with a Bachelor of Arts in Economics, and turned down professional contracts with the Detroit Lions and Green Bay Packers, instead opting to become an assistant boxing coach at Yale University. Even though they didn't want to admit him to the school while he was coaching there full-time, Gerald Ford graduated from Yale Law School in 1941.

Not long after his graduation, on December 7, 1941, the Japanese attacked Pearl Harbor, getting the United States involved in World War II. After the attack, Ford joined the U.S. Naval Reserve. He served faithfully through the war, assigned to a number of duties and ships in the pacific fleet.

After receiving numerous decorations by the military, Ford came home, ran for Congress, and married Elizabeth Bloomer Warren. She became famous in her own right, founding the Betty Ford Center for substance abuse and addiction.

Ford was a member of Congress from 1949, when he was sworn in, until 1973. He was known through his entire congressional career as a modest, humble man who worked to reconcile both sides of the aisle with civility. He gained notoriety in 1963 when President Johnson asked him to serve on the Warren Commission, to determine the true events surrounding President Kennedy's assassination.

Afterward, from 1965, Ford served as the House minority leader for the Republican Party. A House minority leader is the highest-ranking member of Congress for the party not in power, and he served in that position until he was appointed vice president in 1973.

Richard Nixon's original running mate and vice president, Spiro Agnew resigned in disgrace. He was charged with the crimes of tax evasion and money laundering, to which he pled no contest in court. Pleading no contest is right in the middle, between innocent and guilty. You're not admitting guilt, but neither are you interested in proving your innocence. While it's not the same as pleading guilty, you're still responsible for the consequences of the crime as though you were. Spiro Agnew took $29,500 in bribes as governor of Maryland, and he felt the best way to handle his position as vice president was to step down.

This was the first time a vice president had resigned from office since the passage of the Twenty-fifth Amendment to the Constitution, which gives the president the authority to choose a new vice president in the case of a vacancy. Congress has the ability to approve the president's choice. President Nixon went to Congress asking for advice, and the name they suggested for Agnew's replacement was Gerald Ford.

Some accounts state that Congress didn't give President Nixon much of a choice, and on October 12, 1973 Gerald Ford was nominated to take the position of vice president of the United States. On December 6th of that year, after the House and Senate confirmed him in the position by an overwhelming majority, Gerald Ford became the 40th vice president of the United States.

Over the course of the next year, the Watergate scandal grew in size, and on August 1, 1974, less than a year after being the first man appointed to the vice presidency, Gerald Ford received a call from the chief Watergate investigator, Alexander Haig. Haig told Ford that evidence was coming out about President Nixon that would lead to either an impeachment or a resignation. Haig wanted Ford prepared to take the presidency if it came down to that.

President Nixon resigned just nine days later, making Gerald Ford the only man to ever become president of the United States without anyone voting for him. As soon as he took the oath of office, President Ford addressed the people of the United States. "I am acutely aware," he told the American people, "that you have not elected me as your president by your ballots, and so I ask you to confirm me as your president with your prayers." He went on further to say, "I have not sought this enormous responsibility, but I will not shirk it. Those who nominated and confirmed me as vice president were my friends and are my friends. They were of both parties, elected by all the people and acting under the Constitution in their name. It is only fitting then that I should pledge to them and to you that I will be the president of all the people."

After appointing Nelson Rockefeller to fill the vacant position of vice president, President Ford made a big decision that would anger many Americans. On September 8, 1974, he issued a full and unconditional pardon to former President Nixon for any crimes he may have committed. That meant there would be no trial or consequences of any kind and Nixon would not have to face the American people for his crimes.

It was a controversial decision, but President Ford defended it, saying that the whole affair was a tragedy "in which we all have played a part. It could go on and on and on, or someone must write the end to it. I have concluded that only I can do that, and if I can, I must."

While executing his duties as president, and looking to be elected for a term of his own in 1976, President Ford encountered two people who would seek to end his life.

The first attempt on President Ford's life occurred on September 5, 1975, in Sacramento, California. A young woman nicknamed "Squeaky" arrived in a bright red nun's robe, hiding a pistol in the folds.

Squeaky's real name was Lynette Fromme. She was a dancer as a child, even once performing on The Lawrence Welk Show, and at the White House.

Her parents moved her around the country until they found themselves in California. In the late 60s, after an argument with her father, Lynette found herself homeless and drifting through California in a deep depression. She soon found herself in Venice Beach, befriending a man named Charles Manson. Manson was a career criminal and songwriter who developed a bizarre theory about an impending war based on a song by The Beatles. Lynette found that Manson's ravings made sense and stood by his side with a number of other young girls as he tried setting his plans to spark that war in motion. After Manson was convicted of murder, Lynette continued to believe in and preach Manson's gospel, drifting around California with other devotees.

She eventually found herself in Sacramento with another Manson follower, and the two of them took to wearing their robes and preaching Manson's beliefs.

On the morning of September 5, 1975, she dressed in her robes, packed a gun, and went to the park where President Ford would be meeting people. After the fact, she claimed she wanted to talk to the president about the California Redwoods, but instead pulled a gun from the crowd, aimed it at the president, and pulled the trigger. Fortunately, there was no bullet in the chamber (though four live rounds were in the gun), and the Secret Service wrestled her to the ground and arrested her immediately.

She was sentenced to life in prison, charged with the attempted assassination of the president. Though she did attempt to escape prison in 1987, she was eventually paroled in 2009 at the age of 61. She's been living quietly in New York since then.

It was only 17 days from the time of Squeaky's attempt on President Ford's life before another shooter emerged.

Still in California on September 22, 1975, President Ford was leaving the St. Francis Hotel in San Francisco when Sara Jane Moore, an FBI informant, shot at him from 40 feet away as a way to deal with the anger stemming from her political views.

A man named Oliver Sipple, a former United States Marine, saw Moore pull the gun, fire once, and miss. He wrestled her to the ground, preventing her a second chance to hit President Ford.

The bullet that was fired missed the president narrowly, coming within six inches of his head. It ricocheted off the building of the hotel, wounding a taxi driver.

Moore pled guilty to attempted assassination of the president and was sentenced to life in prison. She successfully escaped from prison in 1979, but was captured within hours. Moore was eventually released on parole in 2007 at the age of 77, just one year after the former President Ford had passed away from natural causes.

Despite the assassination attempts, President Ford lost the 1976 election to Jimmy Carter. President Carter opened his inaugural address by thanking President Ford for all he did to heal the nation in such a turbulent time.

Ninety-three at the time of his death, Gerald Ford was the longest lived U.S. president.

Scout's Presidential Portrait

Chapter 11

Ronald Reagan (1911-2004)

40th President of the United States

Ronald Wilson Reagan began his career as an actor, a radio announcer, and a film and television star. Perhaps his most well-known performance (outside of politics) was as George Gipp in Knute Rockne, All American, the 1940 biopic of a legendary football coach for Notre Dame University. From then on, he was given the nickname "The Gipper."

RONALD REAGAN

Reagan served during World War II in the army's First Motion Picture Unit, which produced more than 400 training films for the military. Though he worked hard for the war effort, Reagan never left the United States during his service.

He spent a time as the president of the Screen Actors Guild, which is the union for actors working in movies and television. Then he got a job as the spokesperson for the General Electric corporation. Soon after he was let go from his duties at General Electric, he decided to enter the world of politics. Though he was a Democrat through his younger years, Reagan switched to the Republican Party in his later years.

Impressed by the speeches he gave on behalf of Republicans during the early 60s, the Republican Party of California nominated Reagan to be their gubernatorial candidate in the 1966 governor's race.

He governed the state of California from 1967, through two terms, until 1975. His time in office was spent dealing with political protestors, balancing the state's budget with increased taxes, trying to reinstate the death penalty, and putting the unemployed back to work.

In 1976, he tried, unsuccessfully, to run for the Republican presidential nomination, but President Ford won. Ford then went on to lose the election to Jimmy Carter.

Reagan came back to campaign for the Republican nomination in the 1980 election and won, facing off against President Carter for the presidency. He ended up winning with 50.7% of the popular vote and 489 electoral votes.

On January 20, 1981, at the age of 69, Ronald Wilson Reagan was sworn in, becoming the oldest man ever elected president.

Sixty-nine days later, on March 30, 1981, he was shot by an assassin.

John Hinckley, Jr. was a man with mental problems. He became obsessed with the 1976 film Taxi Driver, which starred Robert DeNiro and Jodie Foster. In the film, Robert DeNiro plays an aimless young man who makes an attempt to kill a presidential candidate, but instead sets his sights on killing the captors of a young runaway, played by Foster. Over the course of repeatedly watching the film, Hinckley fell completely in love with the young actress and wanted to be with her desperately.

JOHN HINCKLEY, JR.

When Hinckley heard that Jodie Foster was attending Yale University, he moved to New Haven, Connecticut to stalk her. He enrolled in classes, followed her around, passed notes and poems to her, and phoned her repeatedly. For the most part, Foster successfully avoided Hinckley, and he left the school in defeat and went back home.

Hinckley decided the reason he couldn't attract the attention of the famous celebrity was that he wasn't famous yet, and he wanted to do something to impress her.

At first, he began stalking President Carter with the intention of assassinating him. He stalked him through several states and would have most likely carried out his plan, had he not been arrested on weapons charges in Nashville, Tennessee.

Released from jail and out of money, Hinkley found himself back home. He was treated unsuccessfully by a psychiatrist for a while, but he began to obsess over now-President Reagan. He began doing research on President Kennedy's assassination, regarding Lee Harvey Oswald as a hero.

Just before he made his move, he wrote a letter to Jodie Foster explaining that what he was about to do was in a bid to impress her so they could be together. Once he'd assassinated the president, he'd be an historical figure, they'd be equals, and he could be with her.

In March of 1981, Hinckley took a Greyhound bus to Washington and checked into a hotel, knowing he'd soon have to make his move against the president. While eating breakfast one morning, he noticed the president's schedule in the paper and decided the time was right.

On the morning of March 30th, he wrote one last letter to Jodie Foster, though he didn't send it, and left to kill the president.

That afternoon, President Reagan went to the Washington Hilton Hotel to speak to a gathering of the AFL-CIO, which is the largest federation of labor unions in the entire country. He wanted the support of the unions through his presidency and was speaking to them about their issues. After the speech, President Reagan walked out to his limousine, accompanied by labor officials, his press secretary, James Brady and a score of Secret Service agents and Washington, D.C. policemen.

Off to one side, for about 30 feet, was a rope line of admirers that had gone unscreened by the Secret Service. Standing in the crowd was an unassuming John Hinckley with a concealed weapon.

As Reagan passed by, waving to onlookers, he passed just a few feet from Hinckley, who knew he wouldn't get a better chance than this. Hinckley raised the gun and fired six times in the president's direction. The first bullet hit the press secretary, James Brady, in the head. The second hit a police officer, who had turned back to protect the president, in the neck. The third shot missed, but the fourth struck a Secret Service man in the stomach as he spread his body over President Reagan to prevent him from being wounded. The fifth round hit a bulletproof window. The sixth and final bullet smashed into the armored side of the limousine, ricocheted, and hit the president in his left underarm. It passed by one of his ribs and lodged in his lung, stopping a mere inch from his heart.

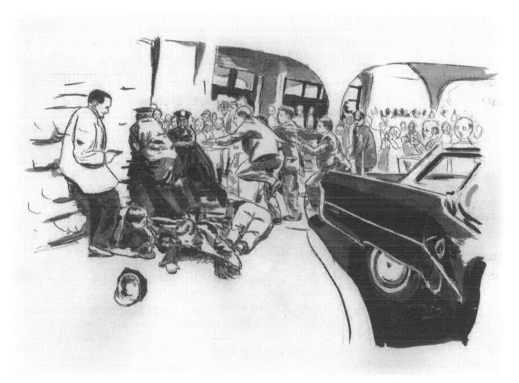

In the car, President Reagan was in severe pain. He thought he'd cracked a rib when his men shoved him in the car, but when he coughed up bright red blood, they knew something was wrong, and they raced him off to George Washington University Hospital instead of the White House.

Reagan walked from the limousine to the hospital entrance under his own power, but he complained of trouble breathing, and then collapsed down to one knee in the lobby. His entourage helped him to the emergency room where doctors cut off his "thousand dollar suit" and found the bullet wound, which surprised the Secret Service who still believed they'd cracked his ribs.

He was in shock and losing blood, so they brought him into emergency surgery. Reagan, still conscious, joked with the surgeon, "I hope you're all Republicans."

The surgeon, a liberal Democrat named Joseph Girodano, told him, "Today, Mr. President, we're all Republicans."

Though he came close to death, the surgeons saved him, making Ronald Reagan the first sitting president to survive being shot. He recovered quickly and became a beloved, though still divisive president until the time his second term expired in January of 1989.

For Hinckley's part, he was arrested at the scene and taken to jail. There, he wrote that his actions were the greatest love offering in the history of the world. He stood trial, but was found not guilty by reasons of insanity. Hinckley was sent to St. Elizabeth's Hospital so that he could be treated psychiatrically, and has been there ever since. In 1999, he was able to start taking supervised visits to see his parents.

The two law enforcement officers that were wounded from protecting the president also recovered fully. Press secretary James Brady was not so lucky. Shot in the head, he survived, but barely, thanks to the work of his attending surgeons. He was left partially paralyzed and with slurred speech.

From his wheelchair pulpit, Brady became an advocate for stricter gun control laws. Ever since the 1980 assassination of the famous musician from The Beatles, John Lennon, the debate over handguns had been raging furiously. President Reagan opposed further restriction then, even after he was shot himself. But it was James Brady's work that caused Reagan to change his mind 10 years later, finally endorsing the Brady Handgun Violence Protection Act (or more commonly known as the Brady Bill). The Brady Bill was finally signed into law on November 30, 1993 by President Bill Clinton, and it required background checks on all purchasers of firearms in the United States. From 1994 to 2008, it's estimated that the Brady Bill prevented more than 1.8 million firearms purchases by criminals and others not fit to carry a gun.

Scout's Presidential Portrait

Chapter 12

William J. Clinton (1946)

42nd President of the United States

Bill Clinton was born William Jefferson Blythe, III. His father was a traveling salesman who died in a car accident just a few months before his son was born. After he was born, his mother left him with his grandparents in Hope, Arkansas, while she went to nursing school so she could provide for her infant son.

Upon her return, she married the part-owner of an automobile dealership, Roger Clinton, Sr.

Though it's been reported that his stepfather was an abusive drunk, Bill took on the Clinton surname when he turned fifteen as a gesture to the man who raised him as his own.

Through his school days, he was a talented musician, singing in the chorus and playing tenor saxophone, but it was meeting President Kennedy as a boy that inspired him to a life of public service. The other key event Clinton described as impacting his decision to enter a life of public service was Martin Luther King's I Have a Dream speech, which he even memorized.

Thanks to his academic work, Clinton was able to attend many schools on scholarships. He received a Bachelor of Science in Foreign Service from Georgetown University. When he graduated there, he won a Rhodes Scholarship to Oxford University, where he studied philosophy, politics, and economics. After that, he attended Yale Law School, and earned a Juris Doctor degree in 1973. That's where he met his future wife, Hillary Rodham, who he married in 1975.

After spending time in Texas working on George McGovern's unsuccessful presidential campaign, Clinton moved home to Arkansas where he became a law professor and ran for public office. He lost an election to the House of Representatives, but became Arkansas' attorney general in 1976.

Two years later, he became the youngest-ever governor of Arkansas at the age of 32. He narrowly lost the position in 1981, joking that he was now Arkansas' youngest ex-governor in history. He won back the gubernatorial post in 1982 and remained the governor of Arkansas until 1992, when he decided to run for president of the United States.

Clinton ran against George H.W. Bush, who had been Ronald Reagan's vice president and successor, as well as the billionaire Ross Perot. As a moderate Democrat and skillful politician, Clinton was able to win the 1992 election.

During his years in office, President Clinton brought the United States through its longest period of peacetime economic expansion in American history.

In 1994, just a year after taking office, there were two assassination attempts on the young president.

FRANK EUGENE CORDER

The first was from an unemployed, ex-army mechanic and truck driv-er suffering from severe depression. Frank Eugene Corder had lost his job, turned to dealing drugs, and did some time in a drug rehab center before he was released in February of 1994. He found himself living in a motel with his third wife and was battling with deep depression and suicidal thoughts.

Drunk on the night of September 11, 1994, Corder stole a small Cessna 150 plane from Aldino Airport in Maryland with the intention of flying it into the White House to kill President Clinton. At 1:49 a.m. on September 12, 1994, Corder found his target and tried steering the plane into the presidential mansion, but instead crashed onto the south lawn, killing himself on impact.

Friends say he bore the president no ill will; he was simply seeking attention. President Clinton was in no actual danger since he wasn't staying at the White House at the time. Since the mansion was undergoing renovations, he was staying at the nearby Blair House, where assassins had attempted to kill President Truman nearly 50 years prior.

Just six weeks later, a man named Francisco Martin Duran approached the fence surrounding the White House, wearing a trench coat and armed with a semi-automatic rifle. Seeing a group of men in dark business suits on the White House lawn, Duran opened fire. He shot 29 rounds at his targets and the White House before a group of nearby civilians pinned his arms and subdued him until the Secret Service could arrest him.

Though he fired an incredible amount of bullets, no one was harmed in Duran's attempt.

He was taken to jail and charged with attempted assassination of the president and assaulting federal officers, among other weapons possession felonies. He pled not guilty for reasons of insanity, explaining to the court that his actions were done trying to save the world from an alien mist, connected by an umbilical cord to an extraterrestrial in the mountains of Colorado.

In response to such a ridiculous defense, the prosecutors brought in more than 60 witnesses to explain to the jury how much Duran hated the government, and President Clinton especially. After five hours of deliberation, the jury found Duran guilty.

Duran is still in a medium security prison, and as long as he remains on good behavior, is expected to be released in the year 2029.

Perhaps the most credible threat President Clinton faced during his tenure, though, was the time he was targeted for assassination by Osama bin Laden. Osama bin Laden was the founder of the terrorist organization Al-Qaeda, and was responsible for funding and planning the 2001 September 11th attacks on America that took the lives of almost 3000 Americans and destroyed the Twin Towers in New York City.

In 1996, President Clinton was in Manila, Philippines for the Asia-Pacific Economic Cooperation (APEC) forum to discuss trade matters. On its way to visit a local politician in Manila, the presidential motorcade route was compromised. Secret Service agents intercepted messages suggesting that an attack along the route was imminent. They found the word "bridge" encoded in a terrorist transmission and redirected President Clinton's limousine away from the bridge it was close to crossing. After diverting the motorcade, Secret Service investigated the bridge to find a bomb planted beneath it. As they investigated the plot, they discovered that it was masterminded by bin Laden, but that information would remain top secret for years.

After the September 11th attacks, bin Laden was forced into hiding inside of Pakistan, where he lived until, on May 2, 2011, Navy SEALS infiltrated his compound with orders to take him dead or alive. Bin Laden resisted and the SEALS killed him.

Later in 1996, President Clinton won reelection in a landslide against Republican candidate Bob Dole and ended his term with a prospering economy and a surplus in the federal budget. He was also only the second president ever (the first was Andrew Johnson) to be impeached by Congress on a charge of perjury. He lied in a sworn deposition about the nature of his relationship with a young woman named Monica Lewinsky. The vote to remove him from office for his impeachment failed by a wide margin, and he left office as the last president to serve during the 1900s.

Scout's Presidential Portrait

Chapter 13

George W. Bush (1946)

43rd President of the United States

George Walker Bush, son of the 41st president, George H.W. Bush, is only the second man to attain the presidency after his father had.

He spent time in Houston public schools before he was put into a prep school in Texas, then a boarding school in Massachusetts. He found himself at Yale University, a C student who graduated in 1968 with a Bachelor of Arts in History. In 1973, after a brief stint in the Texas Air National Guard, Bush attended the Harvard Business School and graduated with a Master of Business Administration.

GEORGE W. BUSH

In 1978, he ran for the House of Representatives in Texas's 19th congressional district, but lost. He drifted through various businesses in the oil industry that mostly folded until 1988, when he moved to Washington, D.C. to work on his father's presidential campaign.

After his father won the election, he moved back to Texas and bought a share in the Texas Rangers baseball team. He spent five years as the managing general partner of the team before selling his stake, which made him a multi-millionaire.

In 1994, Bush set his sights once again on public office and ran for governor of Texas, campaigning on a pledge to reform the welfare system and the tort system, cut taxes, and improve the education system. Bush won an easy primary, but ran an extremely close race against the popular Democratic incumbent, Governor Ann Richards. He won by a very narrow margin, but was very popular, winning reelection in 1998 with an unprecedented 69% of the vote.

In the year 2000, with no incumbent running from either party, George W. Bush thought it might be the perfect time to run for president of the United States.

He campaigned as a "compassionate conservative," setting himself apart from the rest of the primary candidates, whom voters viewed as too conservative. With early wins in the Iowa caucuses, Bush turned it into a two-man race between himself and John McCain. Bush ended up taking the nomination, though McCain would win the nomination in 2008 and eventually lose to Barack Obama.

Facing George W. Bush in the general election was the vice president of the United States, Al Gore. The election was one of the closest in American history, with Al Gore winning the popular vote and Bush narrowly winning the electoral vote.

On January 20, 2001, after a long, bitter recount that was stopped by a divisive Supreme Court decision, George W. Bush was sworn in as the 43rd president of the United States. Thousands of protesters descended on the inauguration, causing the new president to remain in his limousine for most of the parade route to the White House, traditionally walked by new presidents. His motorcade was pelted with eggs as they drove the final stretch. Just a couple of weeks later, in early February, the Secret Service shot a man named Robert Pickett outside the White House fence. Pickett had a handgun and had fired a few rounds at the presidential mansion. It turned into a standoff with the Secret Service. After getting him to a hospital for surgery, he was charged with three years in prison.

The president was inside the White House at the time.

Many were upset by Bush's win, but after the terrorist attacks on September 11, 2001, he found most of the country behind him. He used that goodwill to start wars with Afghanistan and Iraq in an effort to get at those responsible for the attacks on 9/11.

He won reelection in 2004, running against Senator John Kerry from Massachusetts. It was another extremely close presidential election, winning only 50% of the popular vote to John Kerry's 48%.

Because of the protracted wars in Iraq and Afghanistan, American popularity around the globe was at all-time lows.

In May of 2005, the president was visiting the country of Georgia and gave a speech in Freedom Square with the Georgian president, Mikhail Saakashvili. They were each accompanied by their wives.

While the American president spoke, a young ethnic Armenian named Vladimir Arutyunian pulled the pin from a live hand grenade and threw it at the speakers. The grenade hit a young girl, softening its impact, and landed about 60 feet from the speakers.

Fortunately for everyone, the grenade did not go off.

Arutyunian had tied a tartan handkerchief around the grenade, which prevented the striker lever from releasing. A Georgian security officer intercepted the volatile hand grenade while the would-be assassin vanished from the crowd.

The young Armenian would have gotten away completely, but the FBI and the Georgian Government launched an investigation. They found that a visiting professor from Boise, Idaho had taken many photographs of the speech. The FBI obtained all of his photographs and found the pictures they needed to identify the assassin.

After sending out the pictures of their anonymous assassin to the media, the Georgian police got an anonymous tip that led them to Arutyunian, who was living with his mother. They stormed the house, but Arutyunian was ready for them with a gun. A gunfight ensued and Arutyunian killed the head of the Georgian Interior Ministry Counterintelligence Department. Though he was wounded in the leg, Arutyunian fled into the woods of a nearby village. A manhunt ensued, and he was finally captured by Georgian Special Forces.

Forensics specialists matched Arutyunian's DNA to DNA they found on the handkerchief on the hand grenade. They also found an entire chemical lab and stockpile of explosives; enough to carry out several terrorist acts.

On January 11, 2006, a Georgian court sentenced Arutyunian (who had gone so far as to sew his own mouth shut during the trial) to life imprisonment for the attempted assassination.

He is not eligible for parole.

George W. Bush finished his second term in office in January of 2009. Of the things he's noted for improving around the world, he did more than any other president to date in humanitarian efforts in Africa.

After leaving office, he retired quietly to Texas to paint pictures and work on his memoirs. Though he did step back into the spotlight in 2010, after the devastating earthquake in the small island nation of Haiti. That's when Bush joined forces with former President Bill Clinton to raise money for relief efforts to help victims of the earthquake.

Scout's Presidential Portrait

Chapter 14

A Brief History of the Secret Service

The Secret Service is the department of government responsible for the protection of the president of the United States, but it wasn't always that way.

The Secret Service was originally conceived in 1865 by President Abraham Lincoln as an extension under the Treasury Department to investigate and prevent the counterfeiting of money. At the time of the inception of the agency, it was estimated that up to one-third of all money in circulation was fake or forged, making the need for an investigating body acute.

The legislation making the Secret Service official was on President Lincoln's desk the night John Wilkes Booth assassinated him.

Though they mainly investigated counterfeiting, they did help in other investigations for the U.S. Marshals Service. William P. Wood was their first director, sworn in on July 5, 1865. He was considered the best there was at fighting financial crimes, and within his first year as director, the Secret Service arrested more than 200 counterfeiters.

Their first protection job came when they were tasked with protecting the family of Grover Cleveland in the 1890s. Widespread unemployment and economic unrest led to a sharp increase in death threats to the president and his family. The first lady, Frances Cleveland, unbeknownst to her husband, asked the Secret Service for increased protection around the family and the White House. Later, the Secret Service is whom the first lady would call when a number of suspicious men lingering outside their summer home refused to disperse. Convinced they were going to kidnap her children, Frances Cleveland had the Secret Service remove them.

It wasn't until after the assassination of President McKinley that it became a formal objective for the Secret Service to protect the president. That made Theodore Roosevelt the first president with round-the-clock Secret Service protection. And it wasn't until 1951, just after the attempt on President Truman's life at the Blair House, that Congress officially codified presidential protection under the agency's purview.

Slowly over the years, Congress has expanded the amount of people who qualify for Secret Service protection. From ex-presidents to visiting dignitaries, Secret Service protection is available.

After the assassination of President Kennedy's younger brother, Robert F. Kennedy, Secret Service protection was extended to presidential candidates and nominees as well.

After the September 11, 2001 terrorist attacks, President Bush mandated that the Secret Service create a network of Electronic Crimes Task Forces to investigate and prevent attacks on the financial and technological structure of America.

The Secret Service remained a function of the Treasury Department until March 1, 2003, when they were transferred to the newly created Department for Homeland Security.

Over the years, they've given very creative code names for the presidents, family members, and dignitaries they protect.

Here's a list of some of the code names they've given the president of the United States of America:

Harry S. Truman	"General"
Dwight D. Eisenhower	"Scorecard" or "Providence"
John F. Kennedy	"Lancer"
Lyndon B. Johnson	"Volunteer"
Richard M. Nixon	"Searchlight"
Gerald R. Ford	"Pass Key"
Jimmy Carter	"Deacon"
Ronald Reagan	"Rawhide"
George H. W. Bush	"Timberwolf"
Bill Clinton	"Eagle"
George W. Bush	"Tumbler"
Barack Obama	"Renegade"

Here's some code names they've given vice presidents:

Nelson Rockefeller	"Sandstorm"
Walter Mondale	"Cavalier" or "Dragon"
Dan Quayle	"Supervisor"
Al Gore	"Sundance"
Dick Cheney	"Angler"
Joe Biden	"Celtic"

When the British Royal Family visited the United States, Queen Elizabeth II was known as either "Kittyhawk" or "Redfern" and Prince Charles was known as "Unicorn." The singer Frank Sinatra was known to the Secret Service as "Napoleon."

Whatever the funny code names the Secret Service gives to those they protect, they take their job very seriously. And if you've read this book all the way to here, you'll know that they'll take a bullet for anyone they're working to protect.

It's a serious business.

Andy Wilson, Boy Super-genius

"Andy Wilson's built a time machine!" Mr. Gordon said, as he burst into the faculty room in a panic. His bald head was red with embarrassment, and his usually neat mustache was frayed every which way with frustration.

At first, the other teachers weren't quite sure they heard him right. After all, how could a ten year old have built a time machine, but if there was one ten year old on Earth who could have pulled it off, it would have been Andy.

Mrs. Jacobsen, who had been Andy's teacher in the second grade shuddered at the sound of his name. The whistle fell from Coach Stanley's mouth, and Charlie Peacock, the math teacher, dropped his coffee mug on the floor, shattering it.

No one else quite knew how to react to Mr. Gordon, so the rest of the teachers in the lounge just blinked.

"We've got to find him," Mr. Gordon continued. "He could be anywhere."

Mr. Peacock gulped. "Well, that's the problem. He could be anywhere."

"It's my fault he's gone, but I need help." Mr. Gordon raised a finger in the air, pacing to the back of the faculty room.

"How is it you think that we can possibly help, Mr. Gordon?" Mrs. Jacobsen asked as she clutched the pearls around her neck. "It sounds like little Andy Wilson has finally bitten off more than he can chew."

"And how is it your fault, Jim?" Coach Stanley asked.

"We were in history class, learning the names of the presidents and what they'd done," Mr. Gordon said. "He started asking questions, and I told him he'd really need to have been there to really understand it."

Mrs. Jacobsen's jaw dropped open, seeing where things were heading. "He'd have to see what to understand it?"

"I didn't mean to..." Mr. Gordon's face tightened in frustration, almost as though he was ready to cry.

"Where did he go, James?" Mrs. Jacobsen asked.

But Mr. Gordon could not respond.

"James," she repeated, in her shrill teacher voice. "Where did you send him?"

"I had no idea he'd go..."

Even Coach Stanley could no longer bear the suspense. "Where'd he go, Jim?"

Mr. Gordon let out a sigh before saying, "The Pan-American Exposition..."

The teachers who had begun to huddle around Mr. Gordon all furrowed their brows in confusion.

"Where?" Mrs. Jacobsen asked.

"When?" Mr. Peacock added.

Mr. Gordon lowered his head. "Buffalo, New York. 1901."

"You lost me," Coach Stanley said. "I don't understand what you're all so bent out of shape about. So he went to a world's fair in Buffalo in 1901. It's not like he went to the Civil War or the American Revolution or one of the world wars or anything."

"You don't know?" Mr. Gordon's eyes turned soft, looking around at his befuddled colleagues. "The Pan-American Exposition in 1901 is where President McKinley was assassinated by Leon Czolgosz!"

Hearing this, each of the other teachers turned pale.

"Why did he want to see that?" Coach Stanley wondered.

"And how in the world are we ever going to get him back?" Mr. Peacock added.

Mrs. Jacobsen put her hand on her hip and nodded her head disapprovingly. "I told Principal McArthur that we should expel him. 'Andy's going to cost this school a lawsuit,' I told him. Well he's going to rue the day he didn't listen to me."

"I don't care about that right now, Esther," Mr. Gordon told his aged colleague. "All I care about is him getting back safe and sound to the here and now."

"Well, what can we really do," Mr. Peacock interrupted, stroking his chin in thought. "We don't have a time machine of our own. All we can do is wait for him to come back."

"That's not so, Charlie. He left his notes. If anyone is good at equations, it's you. Could you take a look at them and see if you can replicate what he's done?"

Under his breath, Mr. Peacock lamented to himself, "This is why it's hard teaching the gifted..."

Mr. Gordon led Mr. Peacock, Coach Stanley, and Mrs. Jacobsen back to his classroom and brought them to Andy's desk in the front row of the room.

On Andy's desk was a stack of at least 50 looseleaf papers, with various computations written upon each page. Some were filled out with pencil, while other pages were diagrammed in a rainbow of wax crayon colors. Mr. Peacock flipped through each page, muttering to himself as he double-checked the boy's math in his own head.

"Can you do anything with this, Charlie?" said Mr. Gordon, who, for the first time since Andy left, had a glimmer of hope return to his face.

"I'm not so sure. This is utterly brilliant and beyond me, but I can try." Mr. Peacock, speaking through the stack of papers, walked slowly to the door and left the rest of the teachers in Mr. Gordon's classroom.

Coach Stanley held his whistle close to his chin, deep in thought. "How do you know he really left? I mean, he's a kid. It's not like time travel is easy, or even possible so far as I know. He's probably just foolin' you."

"Andy Wilson? Fooling? Ha." Mrs. Jacobsen guffawed loudly. "If he said he was traveling through time, you can bet your bottom dollar that he's done it. Haven't you ever dealt with Andy, Coach Stanley?"

"Not really. He's in one of my Phys Ed classes, but he never seems to show up."

"And have you marked him absent in the computer?"

"Yeah. But it never seems to stick."

"Exactly."

Mr. Gordon snapped his fingers. "I've got it!"

"Got what, Jim?" Coach Stanley asked.

"I know how we can figure out if he was just fooling us."

"And how is that, James?" Mrs. Jacobsen seemed genuinely curious.

"We'll check the history books. If he really found himself in the Temple of Music and close enough to the action, he'll be in the pictures from the event."

Coach Stanley frowned. "Did they have pictures back then?"

"Of course they did. But most anything about the McKinley assassination was a drawing since there weren't any cameras there." Mr. Gordon raced over to his bookshelf, eyeing the spines of each book on the shelf, reading each title in turn until he found the one he was looking for. "Here's the history book we need."

Cracking open the massive tome of American History, Mr. Gordon laid it out on his desk. Coach Stanley and Mrs. Jacobsen hovered around him as he cracked it open, flipping pages, looking for the chapter on the assassination of William McKinley. "French and Indian War...no. American War of Independence...no. Civil War...no. World War I...no..."

"Too far," Mrs. Jacobsen told him.

Mr. Gordon flipped back a few pages, then a few pages more, until he came to a gorgeous, black and white photograph of the Pan-American Exposition. In the foreground was an ornate fountain, round and a hundred feet across, with all manner of people sitting around it and standing around the park beyond that. In the background was a village of intricately designed buildings that had all of the charm of a European temple of some sort. "There. This is where it happened."

Coach Stanley shrugged. "What are we looking for?"

Mrs. Jacobsen was one step ahead of the coach. "We're looking for Andy, Coach Stanley. If he really made it to the assassination, and he made it to the Pan-American Exposition, then it stands to reason that he might be in some of the photographs of the event."

Mr. Gordon ran his finger across the small dots of people in the reprint of the photograph in the book. "It's a long shot, I know, but if Mr. Peacock can't replicate Andy's theorem, then this might be the only chance we can know for sure if Andy's done it."

Mrs. Jacobsen rolled her eyes and grabbed once more at her pearls. "I'm sure it'll be small consolation to his parents that we'll have found a picture of their precious son in a history book. That's like handing evidence to the prosecution. The district will never be able to afford to hire another teacher again."

Mr. Gordon flipped the page. There were no pictures, so he ran his finger along the text, looking for anything that would reference or indicate a young boy out of place present at the Expo.

"You really think they'd sue?" Coach Stanley asked. "Because it seems to me they'd have a hard time proving this was our fault. Or Jimbo's anyway. You're not liable for a horse drowning when you've led him to water."

"That's quaint, Coach Stanley. You're absolutely primeval."

"What does that mean?"

Mr. Gordon flipped the page again, and there it was.

Plain as day.

Across the top half of the right page was the illustration of the assassination of President McKinley. The president stood there in his tuxedo in his receiving line; his retinue behind him holding him up. He'd just been shot. Leon Czolgosz stood there, his hand clutching a gun wrapped in a towel of some sort just fired. Members of the crowd looked on in shock. A few others had the assassin grabbed at the shoulders and were yanking him backward.

The caption beneath was a quote from McKinley, asking the crowd to not beat Czolgosz.

And standing there, in the foreground, was something Mr. Gordon swore he'd never seen in his time as a history professor. It was a ten year old boy in profile.

There was no doubt in his mind that it was Andy Wilson. They had the same profile. The boy was reaching out, toward the president and the assassin.

Mr. Gordon couldn't be sure if the boy was calling out to warn someone or was yelping in shock and sadness. But the eye of the boy, fixed on the scene before him, was resolute.

He wore clothes that seemed only slightly anachronistic for the time period. They were the sort of clothes one would imagine Tom Sawyer wearing if he'd been forced to dress up, which were slightly out of date for 1901.

They'd read as a class The Adventures of Tom Sawyer in the first term, and Mr. Gordon wondered if Andy had decided to visit Mark Twain and the Mississippi river area prior to making his morbid trek to turn-of-the-century Buffalo.

The realization that Andy had, indeed, done it, finally forced a gasp from Mr. Gordon. That gasp forced Coach Stanley and Mrs. Jacobsen to stop their bickering and turn their attention to the history book and the picture of Andy at the assassination.

"My word," Mrs. Jacobsen uttered, stunned.

Coach Stanley could do nothing but gulp loudly like a shocked cartoon character.

"He really did it," Mr. Gordon whispered, trying to wrap his head around such a thing.

Mrs. Jacobsen covered her mouth with an open palm. "But why? Why would he do such a thing?"

"Because I had to see it for myself." A young voice from behind them said.

Each of the teachers turned from the book to the door.

Andy filled a fraction of the classroom's doorway, dressed in the same late 19th century Sunday's best he was drawn into the history book in.

"Andy," Mr. Gordon said. "You made it back!"

Relief washed over Mr. Gordon, and much of the tension he had in his chest and neck melted away. Andy was back safe and sound.

Coach Stanley piped in next, "You had us worried there, Andy. You can't just take off like that."

"We're liable to be sued, young man." Mrs. Jacobsen picked up where the coach left off. "How do you think your parents would have reacted if we'd have lost you at the assassination of President McKinley? They would have most certainly sought a lawsuit."

"Just because my mother is a lawyer doesn't automatically mean they would sue the school, Mrs. Jacobsen."

"And," Mr. Gordon chimed in, "just because your father is a scientist doesn't mean you can just teleport out of school to whenever or wherever you'd like. We're still responsible."

"I know that, Mr. Gordon. But when you talked about it, I really just wanted to see it for myself. And I'd just finished the calculations for my invention, so I figured it was as good a time as any to test out my Time Traveling Box of Doom."

"Time Traveling Box of Doom?" Mr Gordon asked.

"I give all of my inventions names like that. Mrs. Jacobsen? Don't you remember the devices I created in your class?"

Mrs. Jacobsen scoffed, remembering. "How could I forget? There was the File-o-matic of Despair. The Reaching Claws of Scratching. The Document Shredder of Calamity. The Hellfire Gate."

"It's just a naming structure that works for me," Andy said with a shrug.

"But why did you go?" Mr. Gordon repeated.

"Because of you, Mr. Gordon. When you described it, you really made me feel like I was there. It's something all of my best teachers have done. They've transported me to different times and places from the comfort of the classroom. But, for some reason, this was different. When you described the spectacle of the Exposition and the shock of the president, and the idea that real people could get near enough to him to do something like that... I felt I'd been there, but I knew I was missing some part of the experience. You can't communicate in a classroom the chatter of voices in the Temple of Music, or the feeling of excitement as you wait in line to meet the president of the United States."

Andy took a few pensive steps into the classroom. His suit hung heavy on him, weighing him down along with the obvious emotion he seemed to be carrying in his heart. "It was exciting, but also sad, somehow. There was an electric feeling in the room, but I was full of sorrow, because I knew what was going to happen. I looked around for the assassin, but I couldn't spot him in the crowd. And even if I could have spotted him, I worried about saying anything. I didn't want to change time, a paradox wouldn't have been good for anyone. And McKinley, as great an American as he was, was no Theodore

Roosevelt."

Mr. Gordon took in a sharp breath, and raised his finger as though he was going to interrupt the boy, but Andy continued.

"The gunshot was the loudest sound I've ever heard. And then the room was quiet. Deathly quiet. The sound returned slowly, like a pot boiling, and the only voice you could make out for sure was the president's, pleading with the onlookers not to hurt the man who killed him. 'He couldn't have known,' McKinley said... He couldn't have known."

The young boy grew quiet, internalizing the things he'd seen.

Mr. Gordon didn't interrupt. Coach Stanley had grown quiet, and Mrs. Jacobsen, as usual, was lost quietly in her own self-importance.

Andy drew in another breath. "You really had to have been there, Mr. Gordon. It was an incredible thing to see, but sad. Much more sad than I'd realized. When they tell you about these sorts of things in history class, it seems so detached from reality. You see the photos in books, you read their names in print, you hear the tales told, but it's so easy to forget that these were real people, never again able to walk this Earth. Never again able to speak for themselves, or witness what's happened after them."

Andy grew quiet once more and made his way to his desk. The boy sat down heavily, like a world-weary, old man with the weight of many things resting on his shoulders.

He no longer looked like a little boy and Mr. Gordon could see it in his eyes.

Some piece of his innocence was no longer there.

Andy lifted up the top of his desk and rummaged around inside, looking for something. The only thing the teachers could see of him was the top of his head.

Coach Stanley, Mrs. Jacobsen, and Mr. Gordon each looked at each other, wondering what could possibly happen next and what they should do about things.

Mr. Gordon wondered how he should proceed. Was this something to send the boy to detention for? How would that look in the history books? That the inventor of time travel was sent to detention for doing so without permission?

Maybe future generations wouldn't think too kindly of that.

The rustling of papers and junk in Andy's desk stopped and so did his search. From behind his desk Andy's voice squeaked, once more a curious child. "Where are my notes? I swore I left them right here."

Mr. Gordon looked to each of the other teachers once more, wondering if they should tell the boy about Mr. Peacock.

Andy's teacher stepped around his own desk and took a few cautious steps toward the boy's desk. "Well, Andy... The thing is..."

Andy lowered the top of his desk by half, and looked up at Mr. Gordon quizzically. "What happened to my notes, Mr. Gordon? They weren't just my homework. They contained the secret to time travel."

"I understand that, Andy. We were worried. And we were trying to find you..."

Andy's voice was calm and cold, and he never lost direct eye contact with his teacher. "What did you do, Mr. Gordon?"

"We gave them to Mr. Peacock. He was going to see if he could find you."

"Mr. Peacock? He's not anywhere near talented enough to use them for—"

And that's when Mrs. Jacobsen gasped.

Mr. Gordon spun on his heels to see what the matter was.

Mrs. Jacobsen stood over the history book. She'd flipped over a number of pages through the book and was staring down at something that caused her a shock.

"What is it, Mrs. Jacobsen?" Mr. Gordon asked.

All she could do was stutter. "I, uh... It's... I can't... We... He..."

Mr. Gordon looked over to Coach Stanley, and he too was pale, unable to form coherent words until he was finally able to muster, "You better come look at this for yourself, Gordo..."

He came back around to his desk and saw what caused the others so much distress.

There it was; a picture in the history book.

Plain as day.

Mr. Peacock. Sitting on a desk with a piece of chalk in his hand. There was an iconic figure at the chalkboard behind him working out an equation. It was a man in a sweater and a wisp of gray-white hair, poking out wildly in every direction. He'd turned toward the camera, smiling beneath a bushy gray mustache.

Mr. Gordon gasped when he read the caption at the bottom of the photo. "Albert Einstein and Charlie Peacock, fathers of modern physics."

This book would not be possible without the generous contributions of each and every one of the Kickstarter backers who supported this project in its early stages.

We are humbled by your support.

Thank you, truly, from the bottom of our hearts.

Friends of Scout

Dartanian
Melanie Moore
Trish Hanson & Brian
West
Fen Eatough
Brett Schenker
Lindsie & Shawn Bird
Mike Torem
J Mitchell
Kelli Neier
Mark Avo
JA Miller
Andrea Levine
Kate Myers, Eric Benson,
& Isaac Benson
David Avila

Sean Pelkey
Alea Garbagnati
Atticus Pryce & Alisha
Moss
Eliz & Riley Anne
Chad Hardin
Bryan Inks
Janine K Spendlove
Jeff Peterson
Curtis H Steinhour
Kate Vander Voort Wilson
David S Danna
Amanda Johnson
Kelly Adams
Wyatt Meffert
The Click Family

Members of Congress

Linsey Jones
Alex Caligiuri
Jeff Ellis
Erika Turner
Donovan Sherman
Ben Henry Hosford
Susie Fernandez
Melissa Aho
John Chovan, Jr.
Jennifer Chu
Shauna Doumbia
Selena Danielle Rossiter
Derek R Bridges
Tiffany Henderson
Benjamin Vander Klok
Kathryn Pressly

Karen Chu
Sara Kilker
Lady Sarah Graham
Rhoten III, Esquire
Tom Whitley
The Vila Family
JB Lajzer
The Distinguished Senator
Andrew Spiering
Bob Michiels
Denitt Perez
Anonymous
Jason Scott
Christopher M Sneeringer
Nathan Pugh
Gina Asprocolas

Senators

Jon Sagehorn
Amber Biles
Stephen Siebert